PROTECTING CHILDREN AND YOUNG PEOPLE
Early Intervention: Supporting and Strengthening Families

Protecting Children and Young People series

Sharon Vincent, *Learning from Child Deaths and Serious Abuse in Scotland* (2010)

Anne Stafford, Sharon Vincent and Nigel Parton (eds) *Child Protection Reform across the United Kingdom* (2010)

Kate Alexander and Anne Stafford, *Children and Organised Sport* (2011)

Sharon Vincent, *Preventing Child Deaths: Learning from Review* (2013)

Julie Taylor and Anne Lazenbatt, *Child Maltreatment and High Risk Families* (2014)

Caroline Bradbury-Jones, *Children as Co-researchers: The Need for Protection* (2014)

Sharon Vincent (ed.), *Early Intervention: Supporting and Strengthening Families* (2015)

Jane Appleton and Sue Peckover (eds) *Child Protection, Public Health and Nursing* (2015)

Julia Seng and Julie Taylor (eds) *Trauma Informed Care in the Perinatal Period: Growing Forward* (2015)

See www.dunedinacademicpress.co.uk for details of all our publications

Editorial Advisory Board

Professor Marian Brandon, The School of Social Work and Psychology, University of East Anglia

Dr Anne Lazenbatt, School of Sociology, Social Policy and Social Work, Queen's University Belfast

Professor Tarja Pösö, School of Social Sciences and Humanities, University of Tampere

Professor Wendy Rose, Faculty of Health and Social Care, The Open University

Professor Trevor Spratt, Director of the Children's Research Centre, Trinity College Dublin

PROTECTING CHILDREN AND YOUNG PEOPLE
SERIES EDITORS
JOHN DEVANEY
School of Sociology, Social Policy and Social Work, Queen's
University Belfast
and JULIE TAYLOR
University of Edinburgh, Child Protection Research Centre
and SHARON VINCENT
Centre for Health and Social Care Improvement, University of
Wolverhampton

Early Intervention: Supporting and Strengthening Families

Edited by

Sharon Vincent

*Reader in Child Welfare, Department of Social Work
and Communities, Northumbria University, Newcastle*

EDINBURGH ◆ LONDON

Published by Dunedin Academic Press Limited

Head Office:
Hudson House, 8 Albany Street, Edinburgh EH1 3QB

London Office:
352 Cromwell Tower, Barbican, London EC2Y 8NB

ISBNs:
978–1–78046–036–9 (Paperback)
978–1–78046–537–1 (ePub)
978–1–78046–538–8 (Kindle edition)
ISSN: 1756–0691

bitlit

A **free** eBook edition is available
with the purchase of this print book.

CLEARLY PRINT YOUR NAME ABOVE IN UPPER CASE

Instructions to claim your free eBook edition:
1. Download the BitLit app for Android or iOS
2. Write your name in **UPPER CASE** on the line
3. Use the BitLit app to submit a photo
4. Download your eBook to any device

British Library Cataloguing in Publication data
A catalogue record for this book is available at the British Library

Typeset by Makar Publishing Production, Edinburgh, Scotland
Printed in Great Britain by CPI Antony Rowe

MIX
Paper from
responsible sources
FSC® C013604

CONTENTS

THE CONTRIBUTORS

Prof **Fiona Arney**, Chair and Director, Australian Centre for Child Protection, University of South Australia

Prof **John Davis**, Professor of Childhood Inclusion, School of Education, University of Edinburgh, Scotland

Prof **Pat Dolan**, Director UNESCO Child & Family Research Centre, School of Political Science of Sociology, Institute for Lifecourse and Society, National University of Ireland, Galway

Dr **Robbie Duschinsky**, Research Lead and Reader in the Department of Social Work & Communities, Northumbria University

Rhoda Emlyn-Jones OBE, Consultant/Trainer Health and Care, Cardiff County Council

Leanne Evans, Family Coach, Family by Family, The Australian Centre for Social Innovation

Dr **David Hayes**, Senior Lecturer, School of Sociology, Social Policy and Social Work, Queen's University, Belfast

Dr **Michael Hoy**, Head of Safeguarding and Family Support, Southern Health and Social Care Trust

Paul Kellagher, Children's Services Manager, Action for Children Early Intervention Family Support Service

Karen Lewis, SA Operations Manager, Family by Family, The Australian Centre for Social Innovation

Danielle Madsen, NSW Operations Manager, Family by Family, The Australian Centre for Social Innovation

Prof **Andrew Pithouse**, Professor of Social Research, Cardiff University

Katrina Robson, Love Barrow Families Project Lead, Cumbria Partnership NHS Foundation Trust

Wendy Rose OBE, Honorary Research Fellow, Cardiff University

Dana Shen, Director Family by Family, The Australian Centre for Social Innovation

Graeme Simpson, Senior Lecturer in Social Work, University of Wolverhampton

Lauren Simpson, Kids Innovation Lead, Family by Family, The Australian Centre for Social Innovation

Berni Smith, Practice Fellow UNESCO Child & Family Research Centre, School of Political Science of Sociology, Institute for Lifecourse and Society, National University of Ireland, Galway

Mary Smith, Lecturer University of Manchester, England

Alison Tooby, Lead Social Worker for Love Barrow Families, Cumbria Partnership NHS Foundation Trust

Dr **Sharon Vincent,** Reader in Child Welfare, Social Work and Communities, Northumbria University

Dr **Gill Westhorp,** Director Community Matters, South Australia

GLOSSARY OF ABBREVIATIONS

AAI	Adult Attachment Interview
ACE	Adverse Childhood Experiences
AfC	Action for Children
AFST	Area Family Support Team
C4EO	Centre for Excellence and Outcomes in Children's and Young People's Services
CAF	Common Assessment Framework
CAFCASS	Children and Family Court Advisory and Support Service
CAMHS	Child and Adolescent Mental Health Services
CPAG	Child Poverty Action Group
CPR	child protection register
DCLG	Department for Communities and Local Government
DES	Department for Education and Skills
DHSSPS	Department for Health, Social Services and Public Safety
DMM	Dynamic Maturational Model
DWP	Department for Work and Pensions
EI	Early intervention
FbyF	Family by Family
FF	Families First
FGC	Family Group Conferencing
FNP	Family Nurse Partnership
FS	Flying Start
GIRFEC	Getting It Right For Every Child
HSCT	Health and Social Care Trust
IAF	Integrated assessment, planning and recording framework
IFSS	Integrated Family Support Service

LAC	looked-after child
NCSR	National Centre for Social Research
NESST	National Evaluation of Sure Start Team
NGO	Non-governmental Organisation
NI	Northern Ireland
NSPCC	National Society for the Prevention of Cruelty to Children
RPA	Review of Public Administration
SAA	School Age Assessments of Attachment
TACSI	The Australian Centre for Social Innovation
TAF	Team around the family
TUSLA	The Child and Family Agency
UNCRC	United Nations Convention on the Rights of the Child

INTRODUCTION

Sharon Vincent

The case for Early Intervention

As Allen (2011) points out there is nothing new about the concept of intervening at an early stage to try and prevent problems emerging at a later date:

> It is an old adage that prevention is better than cure. The philosophy is enshrined in old folk wisdoms – an ounce of prevention is better than a pound of cure; a stitch in time saves nine; a good beginning makes a good ending. The classic public health definition of 'primary prevention' refers to interventions that ward off the initial onset of a disorder, i.e. intervening before damage takes place in a way that avoids the later costs in both human and financial terms of handling the consequences of the symptoms of that damage (Allen, 2011, p. 5).

The Early Intervention Foundation website offers a useful definition of Early Intervention (EI) in relation to policy and practice in children's services:

> Early Intervention is about addressing the root causes of social disadvantage, ensuring that everyone is able to realise their full potential by developing the range of skills we all need to thrive. It is about getting extra, effective and timely interventions to all babies, children and young people who need them, allowing them to flourish and preventing harmful and costly long-term consequences.

Early intervention should not just occur at an early age; it should take place at an early stage whenever difficulties might arise in the lives of children and young people. It is about providing an integrated, coordinated package of policies and supports to address the multi-faceted needs of all children and young people from birth to eighteen years old. While we clearly need to prioritise the early years, and evidence suggests that EI may be most effective in the first three years (HM Government, 2010; Allen, 2011), we have a responsibility to identify and respond to need throughout childhood. As Allen (2011) points out there are 'important things that we need to do for our older children, especially when the first opportunities have been missed'.

He argues that services fail many children because they do not intervene until problems have become too well entrenched. Not only does late intervention fail to achieve positive outcomes but it is also costly:

> More often than not, delayed intervention results only in expensive palliative measures that fail to address problems at their source. It is time to recognise that the prevailing culture of late intervention is expensive and ineffective ... I recommend a rebalancing of the current culture of 'late reaction' to social problems towards an Early Intervention culture, based on the premise of giving all children the social and emotional bedrock they need to achieve and to pre-empt those problems (Allen, 2011, p. 4).

A large body of evidence now demonstrates the pitfalls of not intervening early enough. For example:

- The California Adverse Childhood Experiences (ACE) Study found that there was a strong relationship between early traumatic life experiences (including abuse and neglect, exposure to domestic violence, parental substance misuse and mental health) and levels of violence and antisocial behaviour, mental health problems, school underperformance, lower IQs, economic underperformance and poor physical health in adulthood (see http://acestudy.org for list of publications related to the study).
- The Dunedin Multidisciplinary Health & Development Study found that boys identified as at risk at age three were more likely to have criminal convictions and to abuse their partners at age twenty-one; at risk girls were more likely to become

teenage mothers and to be in violent relationships (see http://
dunedinstudy.otago.ac.nz for a list of publications related to
the study).

- Recent neuroscientific research on neglect has suggested that
brain growth is significantly reduced in neglected children due
to lack of stimulation (e.g. sight, sound, touch) required for
normal brain development and that, if babies are often left
to cry, their cortisol levels are increased which can lead to a
permanent increase in stress hormones later in life, which can
impact on mental health (see HM Government, 2010).

For some children it is not necessarily a question of having missed
earlier opportunities to intervene. Additional needs can and do emerge
at any stage during childhood, and it is quite conceivable that a child
may develop well and have no additional needs in the early years
but may face challenges at school or during adolescence. Important
changes occur at later stages of childhood and services need to be flexible enough to intervene whenever needs arise. Evidence from analysis
of cases of child death and serious abuse suggests that children face
significant risks throughout childhood but the nature of these risks
changes as they get older (Vincent, 2012). Prevention needs to focus
on stopping risks from occurring throughout childhood. We need to
be prepared, for example, for the fact that a violent man may enter a
child's household and change the whole dynamics of the family; or we
may need to intervene during adolescence if a young person starts to
engage in risk-taking behaviour that might put him or her at greater
risk of suicide or accidental death. Investment in the early years must
be combined with a plethora of services and supports to address the
needs of all children and young people throughout their childhood
(HM Government, 2010).

Early intervention is premised on the fact that all children should
be able to get the help they need when they require it. In the past,
interventions have too often been determined by what services are
available rather than need and silo working has meant that services
have not always been sufficiently well joined up to enable needs to be
tackled in a holistic way. Munro (2011) was clear that one of the best
ways to keep children safe and enable them to thrive was to develop
innovative ways of enhancing the quality of help received by families,

to redesign services around children and families' needs and to provide an early help offer through better inter-agency working.

One of the best ways to support children is to help the whole family. Some parents may require additional assistance to care for and meet the needs of their children, particularly if there is conflict within the family or children are displaying behavioural issues.

Children do not exist in isolation from their families and communities. They need to be understood within the contexts of their families and environments. Interventions, therefore, should be informed by a developmental approach that targets all ecological levels. Positive parenting has a positive impact on children, and if we want to improve long-term outcomes for children we must, therefore, support parents (HM Government, 2010; Waldfogel and Washbrook, 2011). For some children, support might need to include providing access to a range of programmes intended to tackle social and economic disadvantage within the family since financial worries, housing issues and debt are major sources of stress for poorer families and can lead to a reduction in parenting capacity (Brandon *et al.*, 2002; HM Government, 2010; Vincent, 2010).

EI can promote children's social and emotional development, which can, in turn, result in improved mental and physical health, educational attainment and future employment opportunities. If intervention is focused on parents as well as children it can also help prevent issues such as offending and drug and alcohol misuse and can increase the number of parents who participate in training or employment (Allen, 2011).

The case for EI is, therefore, compelling. In addition to improving children's well-being, intensive targeted EI is also the best form of child protection. Countries such as the UK, Ireland and Australia have tended to invest heavily in the acute end of child protection, yet evidence suggests that countries that invest in EI have lower rates of reported child abuse and lower rates of child deaths from unnatural causes (Action for Children, n.d.; Vincent and Simpson, 2013).

There is a growing body of evidence that earlier investment, both in terms of age of early support and at the onset of issues, is more effective than specialist support which is offered only once problems become complex and entrenched. Several organisations have begun to collate evidence on what works in EI: see, for example, the What Works Clearinghouse in the USA; the Social Research Unit at Dartington in the UK; and C4EO (Centre for Excellence and Outcomes in Children's and Young People's Services) also in the UK.

Much of the existing evidence on the effectiveness of EI comes from the USA. For example, the Family Nurse Partnership (FNP), a high-intensity, preventative, home-visiting programme targeted at 'at risk' families is a proven EI model for children born to first-time mothers with low psychological resources. Support is provided by specially trained nurses, from early pregnancy until children are two years of age, using methods that build self-efficacy and promote attachment and positive parenting through practical activities that change behaviour and tackle emotional problems. The programme has thirty years of evidence to back it up in the USA and has more recently been implemented successfully in England. Early findings from the evaluation of the FNP in England are encouraging but it is still too early to know what the impacts of the FNP are in this country compared with universal services.

The UK evidence base is, however, beginning to demonstrate the positive outcomes of intervening early. Sure Start, which was based on the Head Start programme in the USA, involved the development of children's centres for those under five and their families. Children's centres offered new, innovative, flexible services, which responded to local need and encouraged integrated working between professionals. They thus enabled vulnerable families to access services that they might otherwise have found hard to reach. Many children's centres are successfully using evidence-based programmes such as Triple P, Webster-Stratton and Incredible Years, which have been shown to lead to positive changes in parenting and improvements in outcomes for children. Early assessments of Sure Start showed mixed results, but the more recent evaluations of fully established programmes have demonstrated positive outcomes for all children from a range of backgrounds (see HM Government, 2010).

The Dundee Families project demonstrated positive changes for families (Dillane *et al.,* 2001) and an evaluation of six family intervention projects in 2006 (Nixon *et al.,* 2006) showed significant success in reducing antisocial behaviour and preventing eviction. By focusing intensively on the whole family workers noted that the antisocial behaviour of families was related to deeper family dysfunction leading to or stemming from problems such as drug or alcohol misuse, poor mental health, domestic violence or lack of parenting; also the projects were found to have far wider impacts on families' lives. The National Centre for Social Research (NCSR, 2009) collected information on families who received family intervention from 2007 to 2012, and year on year the data has shown reductions in a wide range of family problems far in excess of the antisocial behaviour and risk of eviction that the original projects were set up to address. The data has demonstrated reductions in crime, truancy and exclusion, domestic violence, child protection issues, alcohol misuse, mental health issues and family breakdown as well as improvements in parenting.

EI also makes sound financial sense. It can reduce expenditure on highly pressurised child protection services, and as Allen (2011) points out the costs of late intervention are so high that it does not take long for the right EI programmes to pay back their costs many times over:

> ... people who have had adverse early childhood experiences can end up costing society millions of pounds through their lifetimes, both in direct spending to cope with their problems and behaviours and in the indirect loss of output and tax revenues from themselves and those they affect (Allen, 2011, p. 24).

An evaluation of the FNP (Karoly *et al.*, 2005) estimated that the programme provided savings of US$3–5 for every US$1 invested for high-risk families by the time children were fifteen. The costs of the programme were recovered by the time children reached four, because of reduced health service use, lower welfare needs and increased earnings of mothers. The largest cost savings were due to reductions in welfare use by mothers, increased earnings and enhanced tax revenue from mothers, and less involvement with criminal justice by mothers and children.

Value for money in the UK has been evidenced by the City of Westminster's Family Recovery Programme, which assists persistent problem families. The programme costs around £19,500 per family, and early estimates suggested that costs of just over £40,000 per family were avoided in the year during which the family participated in the programme (Local Government Leadership and Westminster City Council, 2010). The evaluation of the intensive intervention projects (Flint *et al.*, 2011) also indicated significant quantifiable cost–benefits from the interventions with a return of £8 of savings per £1 spent. Some local authorities have been involved in the Troubled Families programme, which has focused on getting children into school; cutting crime and antisocial behaviour; and moving adults towards work, by expanding family intervention services, streamlining assessment processes and interventions into a single 'whole family' approach, and providing better coordination of services. Some of these authorities predict estimated savings of more than £20,000 per family (DCLG, 2013).

The structure of this book

Early Intervention: Supporting and Strengthening Families considers both policy and practice in relation to EI. It acknowledges that the move to EI is not just a UK phenomena and aims to look beyond the UK and include developments from further afield. It consists of two distinct but related parts. Part 1 (chapters 1 to 4) provides an overview of EI policy in Wales, Scotland, England and Ireland, while Part 2 (chapters 5 to 8) gives examples of local promising practice in relation to EI in Northern Ireland, England and South Australia.

In Chapter 1, Pithouse and Emlyn Jones offer a perspective from Wales where the aim of EI policy has been to offer a flexible mix of universal, specialist and targeted EI services to support all families with additional needs. Flying Start (FS) comprises a comprehensive programme of support for disadvantaged children from birth to age four, Families First (FF) is for families with children of all ages where there are additional needs, and the Integrated Family Support Service (IFSS) helps families with more complex requirements. Pithouse and Emlyn Jones point out that the approach taken in Wales contrasts with that in England, where recent policy initiatives have tended to focus on a troubled substratum of families.

In Chapter 2, Rose considers the policy context in Scotland, where the national programme Getting It Right for Every Child (GIRFEC) has involved whole system change as it has focused on addressing cultures, systems and practice simultaneously. Although Scotland has a national policy framework for EI, the Scottish government has not insisted on local authorities implementing GIRFEC in the same way; instead, it has positively encouraged them to develop local structures and solutions. While GIRFEC has resulted in better integrated working, earlier identification of problems and earlier support and intervention, Rose argues that there is now a need to ensure consistent implementation across Scotland and to demonstrate that the programme is actually making a difference to individual children's current and future well-being.

In Chapter 3, Simpson offers a summary of the previous Labour government's policies for targeted EI in England before providing a critique of the current Coalition government's approach to EI. England's approach arguably contrasts with the more integrated approaches to EI which are outlined in Wales and Scotland.

In Chapter 4, Dolan *et al.* explain Ireland's family support approach to EI, which is delivered through the new Child and Family Agency TUSLA. They point out that in Ireland the term 'family support' is more traditionally and widely used than in England to describe prevention and EI to support children and families, both within their own communities as well as in leaving care contexts.

In Chapter 5, Hayes *et al.* discuss Family Group Conferencing (FGC) as a promising practice in the context of EI in Northern Ireland. They conclude that the model is flexible and can be used either as an integral component of an EI initiative, or as a complementary approach. They believe it can be adopted in response to a wide range of difficulties and presenting issues at different levels of need and that it is particularly advantageous in terms of its ability to involve parents, children and young people and wider family and community networks in developing plans to address their own issues and difficulties.

In Chapter 6, Vincent discusses a new approach to delivering EI to vulnerable families through Area Family Support Teams (AFSTs) in a local authority in the West Midlands of England. She outlines some of the outcomes that have been achieved for the vulnerable families who have received support from the AFSTs and considers whether the positive outcomes are likely to be sustainable.

In Chapter 7, Robson *et al.* describe the development of Love Barrow Families, another example of a new way of working with complex families in a community in Cumbria, England. The programme recognises the significance of developing relationships and connections with families and local communities and of building on assets that already exist within neighbourhoods. Coproduction principles were important in the initial design of this project and remain key to its sustainment.

Finally, in Chapter 8, Shen *et al.* discuss the Family by Family (FbyF) model in South Australia. FbyF is a peer-to-peer support programme that brings together Sharing Families (who have been through difficult and challenging times but have come out the other side and are willing to share their experiences with another family) and Seeking Families (who are going through difficult or challenging times and are wanting to change something in their lives). In common with Love Barrow Families, FbyF also involve families as partners in the development of the programme, and this has been central to its success.

Key themes

This book demonstrates that previous and current governments and assemblies across the UK and internationally, which are charged with the task of developing effective services to meet the needs of children and families and improve outcomes, have all recognised the value of EI. EI is now a policy priority in all parts of the UK and in Ireland, and key policy reports – outlined in chapters 1 to 4 – have made the case for holistic, integrated services for children and young people throughout childhood. It is, however, worth bearing in mind the point which Dolan *et al.* make in Chapter 4: 'that good policy alone does not ensure good practice'. While policy is important and it is interesting to compare and contrast EI policy across different countries, it tells us nothing about the lived experiences of the children, young people and families that the policies are designed to support. If we want to know what impact EI policies are having on children, young people and their families, we also need to look at service delivery. This is the reason why Part 2 of this book is devoted to considering examples of promising EI practice.

It is also important to note that we need to make sense of EI policy and practice in all the countries represented in this book within the context of current acute social and economic challenges, which have placed a huge strain on children's services. Local authorities are facing severe funding pressures, while families are experiencing additional debt, housing and employment pressures.

Inevitably, child poverty is a theme that cuts across many of the chapters, and it is, perhaps, not surprising that the practice examples presented in Part 2 tend to be focused on particularly deprived communities. Within this context of public service cuts, resources need to be used more effectively. This necessitates the development of new ways of working with children and families, and the practice examples described in Part 2 are all based on new creative ways of working. In times of austerity there is a risk that already restrictive referral criteria might be tightened even further, meaning that fewer children and families are able to access help and support. The Allen (2011) review of EI recommends new and innovative funding mechanisms, including non-government funding streams, to ensure long-term stability and funding of EI programmes and policies. Some of the practice examples discussed in Part 2 are funded in unusual ways and have sought to utilise formal and informal community capacity.

Early Intervention: Supporting and Strengthening Families demonstrates that across the UK and internationally in this context of public service cuts, there has been a clear political imperative for governments to do something about families with seemingly intractable problems, and this has resulted in the development of new innovative ways of working with complex families and real cultural change representing a move away from reacting to problems to anticipating problems at an early stage. This book examines some of the creative solutions that have been developed to ease pressure on overburdened child protection systems as well as improve outcomes for children and families. It provides evidence of more flexible, integrated, multi-level approaches to service provision across the 0–18 age range characterised by:

- a mix of universal, specialist and targeted services that are focused on multiple areas of need;
- the joining up of all services that work with children and

families, including health, social care and education, housing and welfare rights.

Some of the families who are receiving EI services from the programmes described in this book had been recipients for some time, but traditional services had failed to meet their needs or produce positive outcomes. Others had been unable to access services in the past, due to excessively stringent eligibility criteria.

In Chapter 4, Dolan *et al.* emphasise the importance of direct work with families. All the promising practice examples outlined in this book work with children age 0–18 as well as with their wider family. They are offering more flexible services than might have been the case previously by, for example, removing strict thresholds and traditional referral routes, which inevitably served to exclude many needy families. The only eligibility criteria for receiving a service from the FbyF project (described in Chapter 8), for example, are that there has to be an under eighteen year old in the home and that families want to make change in their lives. This has enabled a number of families to self-refer to the project.

The move to working with parents and children together rather than separately has involved major structural changes, not least the joining up of adult and child services and the breaking down of traditional professional boundaries to create a more seamless service for children age 0–18 and their families. The Love Barrow project in Cumbria and the AFSTs in the West Midlands (described in chapters 6 and 7) both involve colocation of child and adult staff as well as colocation of staff from different agencies: in the Love Barrow project mental health workers work alongside child and adult social care staff; while the AFSTs include child and adult social care, family support, youth work, health visitors and welfare rights workers.

Cross skilling is a key theme across the practice chapters, with professionals from different agencies pooling knowledge and skills and learning from one another culminating in a blurring of traditional boundaries and roles.

Although families are receiving support from multi-agency teams most of the programmes have a main key worker for families, who coordinates services and maintains contact with the family. The FbyF key worker can be an educator, a life coach or a social worker. He or she is known as a family coach and is described in Chapter 8 as 'the professional in the background'. Like the key worker described in the FGC project in Chapter 5, the family coach intervenes only in complex situations.

The programmes described in Part 2 of *Early Intervention: Supporting and Strengthening Families* rely on a whole family approach to intervention. This necessitates a full understanding of the needs of the whole family and of individual members within the family before help can begin. This usually means undertaking one holistic family assessment that encompasses the social and emotional needs of all the children and the parents, rather than undertaking separate assessments for each family member. The FbyF project groups Sharing and Seeking Families in terms of their motivations and goals rather than professionally assessed risks or needs.

The new ways of working described in this book have involved service users and communities. Some of the programmes have been located in local areas so they can respond to specific needs and so they are easily accessible by those living nearby. The FbyF project (described in Chapter 8) ensures it has a presence at local events that families attend as well as in places such as shopping centres and playgrounds.

The fact that so many previous policies and programmes have failed to achieve positive outcomes suggests that we might be wise to consult children and families about what supports they really need. In Chapter 4, Dolan *et al.* emphasise the need to hear the voices of children and young people. It is interesting that all of the programmes described in this book are voluntary, have been developed from the ground up and ensure that families' views are central to decision-making. The FGC project (outlined in Chapter 5) aims to empower families to provide their own solutions to the difficulties they are experiencing: the child and their wider family comprise the primary planning group; while the role of professionals is to facilitate the family to develop a suitable plan. The Love Barrow project treats families 'as experts in their problems'. The programme is based on coproduction with service users, and two parents who receive services are on the project board and steering group. Both Love Barrow and FbyF designed their evaluations in partnership with families. FbyF is particularly effective at including children and young people – for example, in role modelling positive family interactions – and children report that this has given them opportunities to develop important life skills. The Love Barrow project has also skilled up service users. The community Timebank concept allows participants who offer practical help and support to others to withdraw equivalent support when they are in need. The FGC project has sought to build community capacity and rely on local strengths or assets by enlisting informal sources of help in the community.

In Chapter 4, Dolan *et al.* identify the need to take a strengths-based perspective in the context of family support. An important feature of the programmes (discussed in Part 2 of this book) are their assets-based or solution-focused approaches to building resilience within families to equip them with coping skills so they can sustain family functioning once support has been withdrawn. Most provide practical hands-on support as well as emotional or therapeutic help tailored to the family's needs, and they address children's cognitive and emotional development as well as parenting skills and experience. This requires intensive support, particularly at the start of the intervention, and in some of the practice examples described in this book workers see families every day at the start of the programme.

There are a number of challenges involved in delivering EI, and many of these are discussed throughout the book. Allen (2011) stresses that successful EI required a whole new way of thinking and cultural change within children's services, but he acknowledges that cultural change is difficult to implement and can also take a long time to achieve. A move to successful EI requires new thinking about the relationship between central government and local providers. It also needs authoritative evidence about which forms of EI are most successful, and about their impact.

Time is a challenge discussed in a number of chapters: for example, the Love Barrow project took longer to establish than had been anticipated because of the time needed to build relationships; in Chapter 2, Rose points out that the implementation of GIRFEC in Scotland has been variable across local authorities and has not been as rapid as originally envisaged; and in Chapter 6, Vincent points out that it can take a long time to ensure fundamental sustained change for families. Allen (2011) points out that because EI programmes can take a long time to achieve meaningful change they may not be attractive to funders who are hoping to see immediate returns on their investment. He argues, therefore, that projects should seek to achieve realistic shorter-term outcomes that could be seen in, say, two to four years.

Measuring impact is another challenge. It is difficult to attribute positive changes to one particular policy or project, and both Hayes *et al.* in Chapter 5 and Vincent in Chapter 6 conclude that long-term impact in terms of lasting change is difficult to quantify. Vincent argues that we need to be realistic about what can actually be achieved through EI and that we must ensure there is an easily accessible route back into EI services for families who may need further support in the future. Perhaps we should also bear in mind one of the findings of *It's Everyone's Job To Make Sure I'm Alright* (Scottish Executive, 2002), the report of the national audit and review of child protection in Scotland, which Rose refers to in Chapter 2: even with high levels of intervention, the outcomes for some children will not be improved enough to enable them to remain living at home. Engaging with hard-to-reach and hard-to-change families is certainly challenging, and we may have to accept that some families will never be willing to accept help voluntarily. Hayes *et al.* suggest that parental mental health difficulties and parental substance misuse may be particularly intractable problems. Some of the chapters in this book do, however, provide evidence that EI can change the lives of hard-to-reach families, particularly when they are involved in the design of services. The overall message to come out of this book is that EI can achieve positive outcomes for children and families.

CHAPTER 1

Early intervention: A perspective from Wales

Andrew Pithouse and Rhoda Emlyn Jones

Introduction

We introduce our chapter on early intervention (EI) for children and their families in Wales with some brief context setting by way of 'key issues' that inevitably influence the meaning and possibility of intervening early in the lives of children and their families. The term 'early years intervention' or EI is typically used to denote interventions designed to improve the social, emotional and cognitive well-being of disadvantaged infants (0–5 years). There are, of course, various definitions of disadvantage but many include, for example, socio-economic status of family, young mother, mother's lack of educational qualifications, lone parent, marital discord, mental health and substance misuse (see Schrader-McMillan *et al.,* 2011). We do not seek to address the immense evaluation literature about EI, child development and disadvantage; instead, we draw briefly on Taylor *et al.* (2013) who review key international sources. They cite growing evidence of effectiveness of pre-school-based interventions to support parents during pregnancy and early childhood. Critical factors (long known) are the quality and intensiveness of programmes, fidelity to programme standards, and programme success in securing uptake and persistence by participants. We also note that population-targeting around behaviour issues and substantive investment in EI have been identified as key success factors by C4EO (2010) who urge that priority be given to language and communication development in particular. The need for more spending on assessment to identify social and emotional problems, better inter-agency working, high-quality pre-school education for 2–4 years olds, better maternity and paternity leave, and more support for all vulnerable first-time mothers via effective interventions (such as Family Nurse Partnerships) is advocated by Allen (2011). As importantly, Waldfogel and Washbrook (2011) note that a critical success factor is to do with interventions that target multiple areas of need that can involve health, social care and education and which address children's cognitive and emotional development and parenting skills and capacities.

The policy context

While much of the policy and debate about EI assumes an early years – indeed pre-natal – response where necessary, we would assert the necessity for supportive family services which can respond not only to disadvantaged infants but to their older siblings and their parents/carers too. Indeed, the discussion that follows about developments in Wales would suggest the nucleus of such a multilevel service to children across the age range as depicted in the Welsh Government's recent ambitious policy *Building a Brighter Future: Early Years and Childcare Plan* (WG, 2013a). The plan seeks to integrate early years policies and services into a single, ten-year programme with the explicit aim of helping to promote a fairer society. However, Wales – like England – has sought to develop its early years provision in a climate of austerity in public service investments that has raised significant public concern (see BBC, 2013) about capacity to assist all but the most pressing cases of children in need, particularly where there are protection concerns. Also, recent policy initiatives in England raise a number of issues for EI, particularly in regard to their application to what are deemed 'troubled and/or troublesome families' (see Allen, 2011) and where this intervention is coupled to schemes, such as parenting skills programmes, with proven validity but which if implemented irrespective of problem context and complexity will have limited impact. An indiscriminate or simplistic resort to 'what works' family interventions is a trend much critiqued by Munro (2011), who recognises that the embedded complexity of family problems often requires a responsive, durable and multifaceted, relationship-based approach. By contrast, narrowly crafted, reductive programmes that rely overly on behaviourally focused, short-term engagement have often failed to deliver the desired outcomes.

There is no doubt that New Labour invested heavily in EI based on a belief that the quality of childcare and education in the early years was pivotal in respect of children's subsequent life chances. The flagship programme Sure Start was launched in 1999, with its children's centres initially targeting pre-school children and mothers in disadvantaged communities. A complex evaluation (National Evaluation of Sure Start, 2008; 2010) ran alongside this project and demonstrated positive impact in some developmental domains for infants and also life satisfaction and home learning for parents but noted that the aspi-rations of the scheme were not met easily, if at all, in respect of some 'hard to reach populations'. However, belief by government in EI in pre-school years continues undimmed as evidenced in MP Graham Allen's Report (Allen, 2011), which incorporates neuro-scientific research about the impact of neglect on infant brain development and how this impels us to intervene swiftly. This imperative to inter-vene without delay in the early years to prevent lasting brain damage has reinforced for some the need to act robustly towards parents in child protection matters.

The wisdom of all this has been very much called into question by Featherstone *et al.* (2013), who question that there is conclusive evidence about the biological embedding of child maltreatment within particular time frames. They claim that such an approach simply ratchets up the relentless climb in referrals to children's ser-vices and subsequent protection registrations and admissions to care. They assert an alternative – a more rounded and thoughtful engage-ment that delivers early and, where necessary, open-ended practical and therapeutic support to children and families and which in some part responds to what parents *say* they need (see Penn and Gough, 2002). Featherstone *et al.* (2013) worry with some cause that a narrow, age-based intervention via some 'manualised', high-fidelity parent-ing programme will simply 'fail' marginalised, hard-to-reach families exposed to chronic interwoven problems of poverty, alienation, lack of skills and living in high-turnover, risk-filled communities (see also Pithouse, 2007). Yet, the idea that services can deploy standardised family interventions and focus these accurately on specific families who display antisocial conduct is precisely what the Coalition gov-ernment introduced in their Troubled Families programme, which was targeted at 120,000 families in England. This particular initiative was, perplexingly, implemented alongside threats to the funding of the preventive capacities of the Sure Start programme in England (see BBC, 2011). We do not dwell on the Troubled Families scheme but note its deployment of an evaluated, multifaceted intervention approach (see DCLG, 2012) about which there are contested claims in the popular and occupational press about its beneficial impact and performance (see Wintour, 2013; Doughty, 2013; Children and

Young People Now, 2014) as indeed there is in the social sciences (see Fletcher *et al.*, 2012). Such experiments across the border in England have not gone unnoticed in Wales, where there has been a series of very different initiatives and policy narratives (see WG, 2013a). These seek to promote a flexible mix of universal, specialist and targeted EI services that aim to support families with additional needs rather than focus on a troubled or troublesome substratum deemed a suitable case for treatment.

In the foregoing we have set out a context, in England, where deep public service cuts co-mingle with new scientific fashions around EI and high-profile, populist initiatives that aim to do something about 'troubling families'. While this may be a selective and unflattering outline of recent events (see Featherstone *et al.*, 2013, for a much more forensic critique of EI and child protection issues in England), it serves to raise the question 'What about Wales?' People may understandably ask is it so very different from England? Well yes and no. 'Yes', like England we have universal, early years, childcare initiatives and more targeted provision for families as we will outline shortly. And 'No', unlike England there is a demographic and public service culture that positions Wales, discursively at least, very differently to England. Here, we might agree with Morgan (2004; 2006) that Wales traditionally returns centre-left governments, which in the view of Drakeford (2005; 2007) has led to a more progressive, universalist welfare settlement and better protection of public services. While such claims were once persuasive in relation to investments in children's services overall in Wales and in tackling poverty in childhood in the last decade (see Pithouse, 2011), the situation has since shifted. The arguments once made about Wales being in the vanguard of children's public policy and services (see Butler, 2011) are left less convincing in the gloom of ongoing spending cuts since 2010, which have necessitated reductions in statutory and by extension voluntary provision in Wales. Indeed, the National Society for the Prevention of Cruelty to Children (NSPCC, 2014) claims that reductions in public expenditure have been accompanied across the UK by increases in demand on highly pressured protection services. This is thought by the NSPCC to have a knock-on effect on EI, skewing it away from prevention and towards protection work.

Thus, behind a once-confident rhetoric about progress on children's rights made in the first decade of devolution in Wales we have seen ground lost in the battle against child poverty (Crowley, 2011) and increasing rates of children becoming looked after and being placed on child protection registers (WG, 2014a). Furthermore, in regard to early years services it is yet to be confirmed whether Welsh spending will match that intended by Scotland and England by 2015 in regard to offering more free and flexible hours of early education for three and four year olds and more free and flexible childcare for eligible two year olds. In regard to those children coming into the care system, Welsh government statistics (WG, 2013b, p. 3; WG, 2014a) indicate some 5,769 children were looked after at 31 March 2013, a marked increase over the previous five years, as there were 4,627 children looked after in 2008. The recent Wales rate of 91 per 10,000 under eighteen years olds in care is more than a third higher than England, albeit there will be regions and populations in England with not dissimilar rates. Children on child protection registers (CPR) in Wales between 2004 and 2014 have risen gradually from 1,937 to 2,952 and with an increase in those staying on the register for shorter periods. The total number of children receiving local authority care services who were neither looked after nor on CPR (i.e., children in need) actually decreased by 4% in 2012–2013 (WG, 2013c, pp. 6–8). There has been a reduction in referrals and re-referrals since 2010, but this has been influenced, to some extent, by corrections made by some local authorities to the way they recorded contacts and referrals and it is not clear how this impacts on trend analysis (see WG, 2013c). What we might note from the looked-after child (LAC) rate is the preponderance of neglect cases and, for some, a relationship between becoming looked after and general deprivation, albeit there is no agreement on what might be the 'right' number of children in care in any particular local authority (Welsh Local Government Association, 2013, p. 31). It is set against this backcloth of public service cuts, highly pressured children's services, devolution and acute social and economic challenges stemming from an ageing, post-industrial society that we must make sense of EI investments and initiatives in Wales.

We do not have space here to compare early years provision such as free early education and free childcare and related EI for vulnerable infants across the UK countries. Indeed, this is a complex task because of different funding criteria and streams, different early years policy frameworks, different age entitlements, different learning areas, and multiple and diverse, parent-support initiatives. Hence, we do not seek to explore this mainstream field, yet note its critical importance in the way it links to and adds value to more targeted EI programmes. In regard to EI providing more targeted family support, there are three interlinked preventive programmes rolled out across Wales. These comprise: Flying Start (FS) for children under four and their parents; Families First (FF) for families with children of all ages where there are additional needs; and the Integrated Family Support Service (IFSS), which supports families with more complex needs. Together, this arc of services intends to deliver a citizen model of EI through multi-agency provision that offers basic support through to intensive intervention for families at crisis point. Their shared core aims are to offset disadvantage and reduce the number of families developing more complex needs warranting statutory intervention (see WG, 2013c). We now turn to the government-funded FS scheme, which intends to be the Wales flagship preventive service for infants and parents.

Flying Start

Wales is the only UK nation to offer a service like FS – a comprehensive programme of support for some of the most disadvantaged children from birth to age four. FS is a multi-agency EI initiative that is neither statutory nor compulsory. It offers 'universal' entitlements to families in targeted areas of disadvantage across Wales that include:

- an enhanced health visitor service;
- free childcare for children aged 2–3 years for 2.5 hours a day five days a week for thirty-nine weeks of the year;
- evidence-based, parenting-support programmes; and (d) support for early language development.

FS was launched by the Welsh government in 2006 and has been operational since 2007/8 with the aim of making a 'decisive' difference to the life chances of children under four in the areas where it runs' (WG, 2013e, p. 1). Data has been linked to other government data sets to generate additional impact analyses (WG, 2014b). The most recent data on activity levels (SQW and Ipsos Mori, 2014) indicates service take-up involving some 23,579 infants in 2012/13. This is some 4,500 higher than the notional cap of 19,000, which was first identified by government as the target population. FS currently reaches 16% of children and families, and by 2016 aims to help 36,000 children, just over a quarter of under four year olds. The programme cost around £40 million in 2012/13, with an annual budget for each child of £2,100. From 2012 to 2015 there will more than £185 million provided to FS to fund running costs and capital for buildings. This investment – when looked at in conjunction with funding for the FF scheme and the IFSSs that we discuss shortly – is significant and comprises a rounded set of specialist interventions for families in need of support (see WG, 2013d; WG, 2013e).

There have been a number of quantitative and qualitative evaluations of FS in Wales since 2007 led by Ipsos Mori and SQW, and these have focused largely on impacts and intermediate outcomes. Long-term outcomes are yet to be realised. The following synopsis cannot do justice to the detail of the schemes on offer nor to the extensive research that has provided a rich baseline to support ongoing analyses. What can be said at the outset is that the scheme is ambitious in its objectives to enhance the children's language, cognitive and social and emotional development and to identify early on any related need. Similarly, it is a core objective to improve parenting skills and behaviour and also to facilitate work and training opportunities for parents via the childcare offer and thereby contribute in some measure to poverty reduction. Organisational objectives include more integrated and flexible services and more effective routing of cross-referrals. What then does the most recent evaluation tell us about the achievements of FS and, in particular, what lessons are to be learnt about EI?

The second wave of a longitudinal survey of 2,116 families with children aged between two and four took place in 2012/13. It was divided into 1,033 parents in FS areas and 1,083 in selected comparison areas matched on factors such as age, family size, type of housing, lone-parent status, education and other socio-economic variables. Parents in FS areas had on average 5.7 more contacts with health visitors (capped caseloads of 110 families) in or outside the home than did comparison areas and, similarly, 4.6 more in-home visits. Parents were also more aware of parenting programmes and also language and play services in FS areas (17.9% and 24.9% respectively). More parents in the intervention areas reported being referred to parenting schemes (16.6%) and to language and play ones (24.2%). Take-up was also higher on both compared to other families at 12.5% and 13.2%, respectively. Parents were able to self-refer to parenting programmes in some FS areas while parents were referred in most comparison areas. Satisfaction with FS was very high with 82.9% families claiming they were happy with the service and around 14% were more likely to rate the quality of childcare as very or fairly good than comparison areas and, similarly, to rate the childcare as good or very good to help their children learn and develop.

On parent and child comparative outcomes, the study led by Ipsos Mori (2013) found no statistically significant differences on parental self-confidence, mental health or home environment measures. Likewise, there were no significant differences on children's outcomes in terms of cognitive and language skills and their social and emotional development or in relation to their independence/self-regulation. As FS areas are the most deprived in Wales, the comparison areas are relatively less deprived and it may be assumed, therefore, that the parents in the intervention group were likely to be at a more advantaged starting point. Thus, to the extent that no notable differences between populations were found might suggest the programme was successful in bringing the families to parity with those in the comparison group. Such an interpretation was advanced with caution by Ipsos Mori (2013) and conclusive evidence for this is presently limited. That said, there is persuasive data about greater engagement with family services than without the programme, which now has a strong reputation. This should generate more take-up in the intervention areas. Qualitative data (SQW, 2013) with a small number of families (n = 60) from across different regions provides rich insights into family needs where isolation, depression, substance misuse, poor literacy skills and relatively little involvement of fathers featured strongly. Service user perceptions were clearly positive across the programme goals. Additionally, data-linkage exercises by the Welsh government

(WG, 2014a) to other administrative data bases suggest in terms of targeting the areas where individuals were most in need that FS does seem to have achieved its objectives in that changes, albeit small, have been detected in health inequalities between intervention and comparator areas.

Nonetheless, it is important to recognise that, in the case of high-need families and high-need localities, there is a limit to what FS can achieve. It is not designed to address complex family requirements or problems of ingrained severity (see SQW, 2013, p. 5). It may well refer parents and children to more specialist help but has no authority to insist they do so. Similarly, by itself FS can do little to tackle chronic disadvantage such as high regional unemployment. In dealing with families with children of all ages where there are more severe inter-personal problems and/or where poverty makes EI essential, there are other services to call on such as FF and IFSS.

Families First

FF is a government-funded programme (WG, 2013f) that promotes EI response to parents and children with additional needs and particularly those affected by poverty. It moves from a child-focused service culture to a more family-focused model. It has three key objectives:

- reduce the number of families in workless households;
- improve skills of parents and young people in low-income households so as to secure better paid work;
- support families to achieve better health and education outcomes for children and to prevent families developing more complex needs.

The scheme requires local authorities to generate inter-agency 'team around the family' (TAF) support in order to capture the range of help that disadvantaged parents and children need. The scheme was pioneered in 2010 and rolled out across Wales in 2012/13; it currently costs annually around £43.5 million (WG, 2013g). FF is meant to act as a catalyst to local service system redesign, and the use of 'learning sets' is a key element in transferring knowledge about successful implementation. It seeks to innovate and improve mainstream provision and the way this can act preventively to ameliorate inequalities that lead to family instability and poor outcomes for children. Supporting disadvantaged parents with a disabled child is a particular FF theme.

Local schemes will have to prove they can enhance the lives of particular populations and the families within them against five national programme outcomes. These comprise:

- securing employment;
- encouraging children in low-income families to reach health, social and cognitive developmental milestones;
- ensuring children are healthy with good levels of well-being;
- enhancing aspiration and education of children in low-income or workless households;
- providing young people in low income or workless households with support to stay on in education or training in order to secure employment.

Setting of key indicators and national impact and effectiveness evaluation is underway at the time of writing. It will be important for local authorities and their partners to demonstrate how they have used funding to develop 'whole family' support that is tailored to individual family needs. Such support will need to be based on an integrated approach that can connect provision across agencies and programmes (e.g. to FS or IFSS or other community support). FF must be proactive, seeking early identification of need and intervention that is intensive, lasting and can adapt to families' changing circumstances. Much discretion will be left to local authorities about how and where they focus support but all are expected to operate TAF and related shared-assessment techniques (similar to Common Assessment Framework/CAF) together with coordinating mechanisms that can refer families outside the scheme to other services.

Early qualitative evaluation by Ipsos Mori and Ecorys was published by the Welsh government (WG, 2013h). This evaluation, which was based on interviews with provider stakeholders and desk research of local authority action plans, suggested that new shared assessment techniques and the use of TAF are leading to more effective integration and meeting of needs. A clear programme steer towards child disability support has helped, in the view of some providers, to coordinate resources better and reach families not previously eligible for assistance. A more strategic approach to local authority commissioning based on local area need analysis is thought to have introduced more coherent, time-limited alignment of statutory and voluntary resources and better monitoring of quality. However, it is likely that there will have been winners and losers in the voluntary sector in regard to their tendering for funding to help deliver local schemes. FF is very much a work in progress; its limited funding is not well geared to its ambitions to improve population level change. In this initial development phase (2012/13) it was noted that, by March 2013, some 1,867 joint assessments had been completed and some 1,553 action plans were in place across the twenty-two Welsh authorities (WG, 2013g, p. 48). These relatively small numbers are expected to increase and do not reflect the full range of day-to-day encounters with families. Nonetheless, the numbers do suggest something of the modest scale of formal engagement with local people and the need for some circumspection about the reach and impact of the programme as currently invested.

Integrated Family Support Services

IFSS is part of the broader support for disadvantaged families with complex needs, and is complementary to the FS and FF programmes. It was introduced in March 2009 to help some of the most vulnerable children and families in Wales. IFSS seeks to intervene early in the sense that families are often in or on the cusp of crisis, and the usual range of interventions have often failed to deliver change. In essence, IFSS focuses on families where parents have complex difficulties that affect the welfare of their children. Pioneer IFSS teams started work in 2010, and by early 2014 every local authority in Wales now has access to IFS teams. The Welsh government invested £1.2 million per annum in six pioneer regions with a target of 400 complex families per year. Each region contains a number of local authorities, and the pioneer team has responsibility to support these in developing their own teams.

The scheme was established as a result of concerns that cross-sector child and adult services had separate criteria, thresholds, cultures and philosophies, making it difficult to coordinate an effective and timely holistic intervention that kept the family at the heart of planning and intervention. IFSS focuses on families with interwoven and often chronic difficulties resulting largely from parental substance misuse, mental health needs, learning disabilities and domestic violence. Each team reports to an IFSS board whose partner agencies are challenged to address the policies, procedures and priorities that may support or inhibit effective interventions. Evaluation by Ipsos Mori (2013) suggests that the board function has tended to focus on the quality of inter-agency relationships rather than the number of difficult policy changes the boards have tackled.

The core team comprises social workers from adults' and children's social services, health visitors, community psychiatric nurses and substance misuse specialists. A consultant social worker plays a key part in case management and skill development across each team. Expertise is augmented by training in what is termed the structured family intervention model. Here, one team member works with one family and is supported by the expertise within the team and its wider links to public and independent provision. Team members all develop their skills via the same intervention model, which has a strong emphasis on engagement and motivation building within the family. The model draws on motivational interviewing, strengths-based approaches such as solution-focused brief therapy, systems theory and family therapy. Families are supported to engage and lower their natural defences, set shared goals, build on existing strengths and learn new skills. Workers engage flexibly so as to involve as many family members as possible in order to establish clear aspirations for change.

The model works on the family's motivational potential for change in often deeply ambivalent family members. There is an intensive Phase One intervention of four weeks followed by less intensive monitoring and support in Phase Two lasting up to twelve months. The workers focus on strengths and competences and seek to transfer skills around communication and problem-solving; they also assist families to challenge patterns of thinking, set boundaries and routines, help with financial management – all to achieve collaborative systemic change. The collaborative approach is deemed essential in generating trust and honesty over risk and designing conditional protection for vulnerable members in the family. Attempting to eliminate risk rather than help people manage risk can lead to non-collaborative approaches and attempts to hide harmful behaviours. The operating assumption of IFSS is that most families are doing the best with what they have and that it is not feasible for public services to somehow 'rescue' poorly functioning families solely through care proceedings, criminal cautions and court. There must be better ways to challenge families and help them change, and IFSS is the practical expression of that perspective.

A mixed methods evaluation of the IFSS at year three was published in 2014 (WG, 2014c) and suggests that awareness of, approval and commitment to IFSS has grown across participating sectors. The quality and appropriateness of referrals from children's services had increased as had the skills and experience of IFSS staff since inception. Evaluation suggests that the IFSS approach delivers positive outcomes over the short term, while the lasting impact of IFSS is not yet known. Goal attainment by families spiked during the initial intensive period and also at the twelve-month review stage; slower progress was reported between these points. Most families interviewed felt IFSS had been successful in resolving fully or partly their difficulties, and most described it as a considerable improvement on the support they had previously received. Staff were viewed as more willing to get to know them and less judgemental, which helped them feel more comfortable to be open about their circumstances. They stated they understood better the issues they were experiencing, including long-running mental health problems, drug misuse, childhood bereavements and trauma.

Key issues highlighted by evaluation were the reasons and remedies for the dip in progress for some families post Phase One. For some families with complex needs, the timing and level of support offered should be re-addressed and different approaches tested. Engaging with hard-to-reach and hard-to-change families remains, as ever, a challenge, and it is likely that some will not be persuaded to participate or are too disorganised to do so. The coaching, mentoring and training of the team and the wider workforce to expand effective practice and build capacity remain a challenging resource matter. The impact of this investment in skilling up the wider workforce is not currently being evaluated, while the improvement in access to and coordination of services are also areas that would benefit from further analysis.

Conclusion

FS, FF and the IFSS share key principles that recognise the importance of helping families rather than relying on protection or surveillance to solve problems – albeit safe care and risk management are very much part of the EI curriculum across these three services. A strong national and local policy interface to support programme roll-out and strong investment in skills and capacities for staff, ensuring clear evidence-based methodologies and focusing on reducing the barriers across services, are providing Wales with a platform from which to build greater integration, further insight and improved outcomes. We await the full results of these endeavours.

CHAPTER 2

The policy context in Scotland

Wendy Rose

Introduction

In 2001, the ministers for Education, Health and Social Justice jointly set out Scotland's aspirations in *For Scotland's Children*: 'Our children are our future. That is why we have committed ourselves to creating a Scotland in which *Every Child Matters*; where every child, regardless of their family background, has the best possible start in life' (Scottish Executive, 2001, Foreword). The report starts with a hard look at the reality of a million children's lives in Scotland: a third of Scottish children begin their lives in poverty; one in ten households is 'multiply deprived'; and one in a hundred is 'seriously deprived' (ibid., p. 13). Its conclusion is that current service arrangements are 'failing some of our most disadvantaged children ... the one option that is *not* available is to do nothing' (ibid., p. 19). The report makes a compelling case for widespread change and improvement.

As a result, Scotland has been on a journey over the last fourteen years, the foundations for which were laid down in *For Scotland's Children* (Scottish Executive, 2001). This chapter examines the route the journey has taken, how Scotland has been working to fulfil its commitment to its children and how EI has been given a central role in improving children's outcomes, with the emphasis on ensuring children get the help they need when they need it. There are ways in which policy development in Scotland has been markedly different from other countries of the UK although facing similar challenges, and these variations include the adoption of whole system change, taking a universal approach to all children and building on the universal services of health and education. The stability and coherence underlying policy development over this period are unusual and have had an important impact. Inevitably, there are achievements and challenges in Scotland's approach, which are discussed.

The chapter concludes that the scale of change has gone far wider and deeper than originally envisaged in 2001, and has permeated every aspect of central and local government policy concerning the well-being of children as well as the practice of every agency in touch or working with children and their families. Ensuring that all children and young people are fully supported 'as they grow and develop into successful learners, confident individuals, effective contributors and responsible citizens' (Scottish Government, 2012a, p. 3) remains a challenge for present and future governments, for service providers and for communities across Scotland. Powerful leadership as well as adequate resources and local commitment are still key factors in ensuring that these policies are effectively embedded in local systems and practice, as part of a wider policy agenda for improving the well-being of all Scotland's citizens.

Giving every child the best possible start in life

The report *For Scotland's Children* (Scottish Executive, 2001) was the result of an extensive collaborative exercise in gathering and analysing evidence by stakeholders from across Scotland working together and with Scottish Executive officials. The consequence of this was that, when the findings were published, there was a considerable degree of consensus about the proposals for the way forward. As Aldgate (2010, p. 55) observes, the report provides: 'a blueprint for an integrated approach to children's services ... which set out a policy base to give every child in Scotland "the best possible start in life" '.

The key features of the blueprint are that children's services should be considered as a single service system, facilitating a new way of working across existing agencies and organisational structures. It does not advocate major organisational change or restructuring of services to achieve this. However, at a strategic level in each area, it is essential that local authorities, NHS Boards and other partners are actively working together and agree a joint local children's service plan detailing the way forward and the priorities for action and resource investment. Inclusive access by all children to universal services needs to be ensured and, wherever possible, children's needs met from within health and education services. Making a difference to the outcomes for children requires early sharing of information and communication of concerns, a single modular assessment format for use by all agencies, and a Named Person for children and families, from either health or education, who acts as an information/reference point and coordinator of arrangements for earlier and more effective intervention. Some children require extra help and support, and additional services should be targeted to meet their specific needs.

While these proposals would be building on examples of good practice already being developed in different parts of Scotland, the report (Scottish Executive, 2001) acknowledges that such a plan requires cross-government effort and powerful leadership to drive it forward and to achieve consistency and commitment in its implementation across Scotland.

The relationship between these proposed changes and combating child poverty and poor child outcomes is clearly drawn by ministers in their Foreword to the report: 'Delivering high-quality services to all children is key to combating child poverty in Scotland, and to ensuring all children have the necessary support to widen their opportunities for the future' (Scottish Executive, 2001). Tackling child poverty and wider socio-economic deprivation and health inequalities in Scotland continues to be high priority for the Scottish government (Scottish Government, 2014b) and a theme to which the Chief Medical Officer has returned in his annual reports on Health in Scotland (see Scottish Government, 2010 and 2012b). In his annual report for 2011 he stated:

> If we are to have the greatest chance of influencing the determinants of health and well-being, we should focus efforts on actions to improve the quality of care for children and families. We should start by making efforts to ensure a safe and healthy pregnancy, a nurturing childhood and support for families in providing such circumstances in which to bring up children (Scottish Government, 2012, p. 10).

Improving protection for Scotland's children

An integral part of promoting children's well-being is in ensuring that they are protected from harm and grow up in a safe environment. These issues are addressed in a second major national report, *'It's Everyone's Job To Make Sure I'm Alright'* (Scottish Executive, 2002). The aim of this review was to promote the reduction of abuse and neglect of children and to improve the services for those children. The report also pays: 'particular attention to the needs of the small number of children whose family or environmental circumstances are so poor that their future well-being is placed at serious risk' (Scottish Executive, 2002, p. 4).

In its conclusions, the report highlights the finding that: 'good practice included the provision of help to parents and children as and when it was needed, timely responses, early thought and preparation, and properly addressing the source of the risk'. It also acknowledges that, even with high levels of intervention, the outcomes for some children cannot always be sufficiently improved for them to remain living at home (Scottish Executive, 2002, p. 13). The report reflects and reinforces many of the findings of *For Scotland's Children* (Scottish Executive, 2001), strongly recommending coordinated strategic collaboration across local agencies, underpinned by children's services: '[Plans] should be led by a children's rights rather than a public service perspective and should promote <u>every</u> child's rights to life, health, decency and development' (Scottish Executive, 2002, p. 17). Recommendations are also focused on the level of agency practice and on improvement in assessing children's risks and needs, especially of those children at greater risk of harm from family or environmental circumstances (ibid., p. 17).

These two reviews identify themes and principles that have continued to inform and shape the direction taken by Scotland and the development of policy affecting children and young people. The issues they identify are not distinctive to Scotland alone. Other countries in the UK and internationally have also been struggling to find new responses to the same challenges of how to improve children's outcomes and develop effective integrated service responses to meeting the needs of children and families. In England and Wales, the *Framework for the Assessment of Children in Need and Their Families* (Department of Health *et al.*, 2000) and, in Northern Ireland, *Understanding the Needs of Children in Northern Ireland* (UNOCINI, 2008) were being developed in a similar time period and were rooted in the same theories and knowledge about children's development within an ecological perspective, and the importance of keeping the focus on the child while working to strengthen families and communities to support children and young people (see Rose, 2010).

However, Scotland took a broader, cross-government stance from the start, and its approach builds on and is reflected in a wide range of policies and strategies for all children and young people (including those who may have additional support needs). These include policies in education (*A Curriculum for Excellence*, Scottish Executive, 2004a), child protection (*Protecting Children and Young People: The Charter*, Scottish Executive, 2004b), health (*Health for All Children 4: Guidance on Implementation in Scotland*, Scottish Executive, 2005b: *Better Health, Better Care: Action Plan*, Scottish Government, 2007) and early years (*The Early Years Framework*, Scottish Government and COSLA, 2008; *Early Years Framework: Progress So Far*, Scottish Government and COSLA, 2011).

A whole system approach

As policy work on improving children's services in Scotland progressed following *For Scotland's Children* (Scottish Executive, 2001), the need for change at all levels and in all agencies working with children and families became evident. It was recognised that a whole system approach was required, which addressed changes in culture, systems and practice simultaneously. There had to be changes in professional cultures, systems in place to support variations in policy and practice, and effective integrated, multi-agency, child-centred practice created. It was also recognised that developments of this breadth and magnitude would necessitate long-term commitment (Stradling *et al.*, 2009).

In 2005, the Scottish Executive launched its ambitious national programme, Getting It Right For Every Child (GIRFEC), with the aim of improving the outcomes for all children and young people in Scotland. As part of a review of the Scottish Children's Hearings System, a national integrated assessment, planning and recording framework (IAF) was introduced; this was a critical step in reforming the children's support system. It was aiming at earlier identification of concerns and earlier intervention with 'the intention that children receive the help they need when they need it' (Scottish Executive, 2005a). From this point, GIRFEC began to evolve and its application 'was subsequently widened to be used in practice with all children' by all services and agencies working with children and families, to deliver a coordinated approach that was appropriate, proportionate and timely (Aldgate, 2010, p. 33; see also Stradling *et al.*, 2009).

A shared concept of children's well-being was developed, using a common language and tools based on well-being across all services, which form a common coordinated framework together with a National Practice Model for assessing how well a child is doing and what needs to change to improve their outcomes (Aldgate, 2010). Eight well-being indicators – central to the framework and practice model – are that children should be 'safe, healthy, active, nurtured, achieving, respected, responsible and included' (Scottish Government, 2008).

From vision to practice

The next stage involved the development and refinement of GIRFEC and testing it out in practice. Highland Council with its partner agencies was already in the vanguard of developing children's services along the lines advocated in *For Scotland's Children* (Scottish Executive, 2001) and evaluating its progress (see Stradling and Mac-Neil, 2007). Highland was designated a pathfinder by the Scottish Executive from 2006, with the task of applying GIRFEC across Inverness. The Scottish Executive explained its approach: 'We will take this forward incrementally, learning as we go and identifying the barriers to change at local and national level. All the learning from this and other pilots will be written up to assist in national roll-out' (Scottish Executive, 2006, p. 2).

In addition to the whole system pathfinder in Highland, two other local authorities (Edinburgh and Lanarkshire) became learning partners as part of the development programme and they contributed to 'learning as we go'. A further pathfinder project was established in four different areas from 2007, designed to test out the implementation of the GIRFEC approach in response to a single issue or theme – in this case, meeting the needs of children and young people living with or affected by domestic abuse (Stradling *et al.*, 2009, p. v).

The Scottish Executive provided project management funding but the pathfinder projects were to be taken forward on 'a resource neutral basis' (Scottish Executive, 2006, p. 2). Although this might suggest limited financial liability on the part of the Executive, in reality the stakes were high. The policy intentions and the progress of the pathfinders and other partners were high profile and widely publicised in Executive-led roadshows with stakeholders across Scotland and by other regular communication. The level of project scrutiny was demanding but accompanied by an equally high level of ministerial and official commitment and determination to succeed. (A detailed discussion of how the pathfinder approach worked can be found in the evaluation by Stradling *et al.*, 2009.)

In November 2008, the Scottish Government published and issued widely *A Guide to Getting It Right For Every Child*, marking a significant shift from the development phase to national implementation. The guide set out the framework and 'emerging practice model', and all practitioners and agencies working with children were encouraged to consider how the guide and model might be incorporated into their work with children (Scottish Government, 2008).

Getting it right for every child – the framework

The GIRFEC approach is rooted in the United Nations Convention on the Rights of the Child (UNCRC) and informed by knowledge and research, legislation, standards, professional expertise and the experience of children and families, providing a common platform for promoting the well-being of children and young people (Scottish Government, 2008, pp. 15–17; Scottish Government, 2012a, pp. 7–8; Scottish Government, 2013a).

The approach has an explicit set of values and principles, based on an ecological understanding of children's development that emphasises promoting strengths and resilience and the importance of families and friendships, schools and communities in supporting children growing up. It is also rooted in children's rights and their competence to contribute to and be heard about decisions that affect them. A basic principle is that there will be more chance of improving children's outcomes if children and families get the services they need when they require them and in the most appropriate way.

Ten core components of GIRFEC are identified (see Table 2.1) which, with the values and principles, bring meaning and relevance at a practice level to single-agency, multi-agency and inter-agency working across the whole of children's services and can be applied in any setting and circumstance where people are working with children and young people (Scottish Government, 2012a, p. 7).

Table 2.1 GIRFEC core components

1. a focus on improving outcomes for children, young people and their families based on a shared understanding of well-being;
2. a common approach to gaining consent and to sharing information where appropriate;
3. an integral role for children, young people and families in assessment, planning and intervention;
4. a coordinated and unified approach to identifying concerns, assessing needs, and agreeing actions and outcomes, based on the Well-being Indicators;
5. streamlined planning, assessment and decision-making processes that lead to the right help at the right time;
6. consistent high standards of cooperation, joint working and communication where more than one agency needs to be involved, locally and across Scotland;
7. a Named Person for every child and young person, and a Lead Professional (where necessary) to coordinate and monitor multi-agency activity;
8. maximising the skilled workforce within universal services to address needs and risks as early as possible;
9. a confident and competent workforce across all services for children, young people and their families;
10. the capacity to share demographic, assessment and planning information — including electronically — with and across agency boundaries (Scottish Government, 2012a, p. 7).

Building a network of support around each child or young person

The underlying premise of the GIRFEC framework, derived from the values and principles discussed earlier, is that each and every child needs the support of their families and/or carers and the universal services of health and education to ensure that they are safe, healthy, achieving, nurtured, active, respected, responsible and included, so they can grow and develop and reach their full potential. Many children will draw the help they need from their local community. Only when support from the family and community and the universal services can no longer meet their needs will targeted and specialist help be called on or when immediate action is necessary to keep children and young people safe. A fundamental building block, therefore, is 'to have a network of support in place to promote well-being so that children and young people get the

Figure 2.1 Building a network of support (Source: Scottish Government, 2012a).

right help at the right time' (illustrated in Figure 2.1 in a diagram 'which reads from the inside out', Scottish Government, 2012a, p. 12). Key to mobilising this network is the contact between children and families with frontline professionals in health and education.

A Named Person for every child

To facilitate earlier intervention and the delivery of support where and when it is needed, the concept of a Named Person for every child in the universal services was formulated and formalised during the development phase of GIRFEC (Scottish Government, 2012, p. 13) (see Table 2.2).

As discussed earlier in the chapter, a named individual for every child is recommended in *For Scotland's Children* (Scottish Executive, 2001) but it has proved to be one of the more contested areas in GIRFEC and has taken time to become embedded in practice. It was introduced during the pathfinder project in Highland:

Table 2.2 The role of the Named Person

The GIRFEC approach includes a Named Person for every child, from birth (or sometimes before) until they reach eighteen.

In most cases, the Named Person will not have to do anything more than they normally do in the course of their day-to-day work. The major difference will be that they use the National Practice Model as a starting point for recording both routine information about a child or young person and for when they have particular concerns.

Most children and young people get all the help and support they need from their families, from teachers and health practitioners, and from their wider communities. But some may need extra help and that is where the Named Person comes in.

Depending on the age of the child or young person, a health visitor or teacher usually takes the role of Named Person. This means that the child and their family have a point of contact who can work with them to sort out any further help, advice or support if they need it.

Once a concern has been brought to their attention, the Named Person — who will be the first point of contact for the child and their family — needs to take action, help or arrange for the right help in order to promote the child's development and well-being.

Referring to the eight Well-being Indicators, they will need to ask these five questions:
- What is getting in the way of this child or young person's well-being?
- Do I have all the information I need to help this child or young person?
- What can I do now to help this child or young person?
- What can my agency do to help this child or young person?
- What additional help — if any — may be needed from others?

The Named Person also needs to help children and families feel confident they can raise concerns and talk about their worries to people who will listen and respect their point of view and work with them to sort things out. Above all, they will ensure that the child or young person's views are listened to and that the family (where appropriate) is kept informed (Scottish Government, 2012, p. 13)

> The universal services in Highland have agreed that every child and young person will have a Named Person in health or education if they are of school age. These individuals will be responsible for making sure that the child has the right help in place to support his or her development and well-being ... (Stradling *et al.*, 2009, p. 56)

However, it was not included in the first *Guide to Getting It Right For Every Child* (Scottish Government, 2008). With accumulated experience of its working successfully in practice in Highland and evidence that children's needs were being identified at an earlier stage by Named Persons (Stradling *et al.*, 2009, p. 61), there was more confidence to allow the Scottish government, in its *Guide* to *Implementing Getting It Right For Every Child* (Scottish Government, 2010b), to support on a national basis the concept of a Named Person in health or education as the first point of contact for children and families.

There are many reasons why professionals in health and education might have reservations about being a Named Person – additional responsibilities, greater volume of work, more knowledge and training required, more recording, more accountability, finding themselves in difficult situations without relevant support and guidance, and managing the role as, or relationship with, a Lead Professional in more complex cases involving several agencies. In reality, many professionals in health and midwifery already undertake the Named Person tasks as part of their day-to-day work and there are many teachers and guidance staff in schools who provide information, support and pastoral care for individual pupils and their families. However, Stradling *et al.* (2009, p.58) observe that, in the Highland pathfinder, the Named Person was initially proving to be a complex role and there were new aspects to the role emerging as the protocols and practice bedded in, engendering 'a great deal of debate and solution-focused negotiation'.

Many of the early concerns have not been realised and rather different perspectives are being voiced as the role has become more embedded. A parent says:

> For me, the concept of the Named Person works because I will have a named and known professional with whom I can communicate any concerns or share any information. Parents are often frustrated and confused by not knowing who to contact or by professional teams changing frequently. At times of pressure or concern, clarity will be a real benefit (Scottish Government, 2013b, p. 5).

Named Persons are now able to draw on their experience and describe the value of the role in very specific ways.

A bond of trust — a closer look at the role of the Named Person

Katrina Szimaitis, an experienced health visitor based in Prestwick, says: 'The concept behind the Named Person has been around for a long time. It is a strong nurse-client relationship that means families have someone they can rely on for encouragement, advice, support and professional guidance'. She cites the wider and more consistent recognition and valuing of her health visitor role among other professions, giving as examples how local police now tell her about every domestic incident they attend involving any family on her caseload and local hospitals inform her about any visits to accident and emergency so she can offer appropriate advice and support. She also describes her response to a mother with concerns about her toddler's behaviour which were confirmed by Katrina. This led to Katrina arranging an early nursery place to increase social skills, and appointments with a child psychologist, paediatrician and speech and language therapist. The family is relieved at the extra support their child is receiving and a child's plan for the toddler has been drawn up by the health visitor to set out 'how different services will be able to support the family and Katrina hopes that this early action will get [the child] back on track' (summarised from an article in Scottish Government, 2013b, pp. 7–8)

The Named Person exemplifies the transformational change that GIRFEC requires. It challenges traditional professional cultures in health, education, police and social work where a child's difficulties may be characterised as: 'oh, that's a social work problem' or 'that's a health problem'. A child-centred approach asks for a shift away from what Stradling *et al.* (2009, p. 8) describe as 'a sequential model of joint working' to 'a parallel collaboration model' to enable the network of support to work effectively for the child and family. The Named Person role highlights the need for different inter-agency protocols and systems to be negotiated and agreed. Multi-agency practice has to ensure active and responsive engagement with children and families, information is shared on a functional basis, liaison between services becomes standard practice, and practitioners feel fully supported in their roles.

To legislate or not to legislate

The Scottish government's approach to the implementation of GIRFEC has been one of encouragement and engagement with Community Planning Partnerships and other agencies across Scotland: 'It is recognised that [GIRFEC] will not be implemented in the same way or at the same pace in every part of Scotland … Local structures and local solutions will always be necessary' (Scottish Government, 2010b, Minister's Foreword). This approach is somewhat at variance with a 'command and control' approach to policy implementation used in some other countries. Apart from a philosophical difference in approach, it can be argued that it reflects the sensitive relationship between national government and local partners in Scotland and the agreement to a 'consensus and collaboration' approach to delivery of change that has developed (Scottish Government and COSLA, 2011).

However, concern has grown in government that progress on implementation of GIRFEC has been variable and not as rapid as originally envisaged, despite reports that all Community Planning Partnerships were working actively to deliver the GIRFEC approach (Scottish Government, 2014a). It was proposed to enshrine key elements of GIRFEC in the Children and Young People (Scotland) Act 2014 in order ensure greater consistency of implementation nationally. Whether a Named Person for every child should be included as a mandatory requirement in the Act was hotly debated at the Bill stage, resulting in a public briefing to Members of the Scottish Parliament (MSPs) from Children in Scotland and twelve other organisations as signatories, concluding: 'We urge all MSPs to continue to support GIRFEC and in particular the principle of the Named Person at Stage 3 of the Children and Young People Bill' (Children in Scotland, 2014). A Named Person for every child is now a provision of the Act, as is a single planning system for each child and new statutory functions for sharing information (Scottish Government, 2014a).

Conclusion

GIRFEC has become the overarching policy framework for all services delivered to children in Scotland. It has been described by the Minister for Children and Early Years as: 'the golden thread that knits together our policy objectives for children and young people' (Scottish Government, 2010a). GIRFEC is now seen as 'a key policy driver to improve outcomes for all children' (Scottish Government, 2014a). Despite a change of government in 2007, it has continued to enjoy cross-party support in the Scottish Parliament and in local authorities (Children in Scotland, 2014). GIRFEC is now enshrined in legislation in the Children and Young People (Scotland) Act 2014. This continuity has provided Scotland with an unusual degree of policy coherence and stability, the value of which is not to be underestimated. Electoral changes are often characterised by jettisoning the previous administration's policies and starting afresh (literally in England in May 2010, as the banners and logos for *Every Child Matters* disappeared overnight from Sanctuary Buildings, the headquarters of the Department for Education, heralding a new set of policy directions and priorities under the Coalition government).

The challenge is to achieve consistent implementation of GIRFEC in every Community Planning Partnership area across Scotland and to find out if it is making a difference to children's well-being now and their well-becoming in the future. There may be evidence of better integrated working, earlier identification of problems and earlier support and intervention. However, information about the impact on individual children's well-being needs to be carefully recorded and evaluated. Improving the outcomes for all Scotland's children remains a priority aspiration and a new provision in the Children and Young People (Scotland) Act 2014 places a duty on Community Planning Partnerships to report on the outcomes of all children in their local communities.

CHAPTER 3

Strengthening families? From Labour to the Coalition (1997–2014)

Graeme Simpson

Introduction

EI as a concept has gained considerable political and intellectual momentum in England during the last seventeen years. The chapter seeks to examine the different ways that it has emerged in terms of public policy from Labour's first administration in 1997. ('Labour' is used throughout the chapter as it remained the official name of the party in government, even though it was 'rebranded' 'New Labour' by Tony Blair and was used to distinguish the 'modernising' wing in the party from the more traditional wing of the party or 'old' Labour. The term is frequently used by commentators to refer to the Labour party under Tony Blair's leadership.)

An outline of Labour's core policies for families and EI in England from 1997 to 2010 establishes the context for the subsequent discussion of the Conservative and Liberal Democrat coalition government (henceforth the 'Coalition') policies from 2010 onwards. Through a discussion of the Coalition's Troubled Families programme and the Children and Families Act 2014, key themes are analysed in relation to children and EI. Fiscal policy and its 'austerity measures' are significant in the analysis, which highlights a reframing of the debates around EI.

While their programmes of EI remain, the background to the arguments in this chapter comprise the abandonment of Labour's targets for reducing child poverty, and the consequences of the Coalition's 'austerity policy', which impact disproportionately on low-income groups and their children. Despite policies that promise support, the Coalition government has done little to provide children from these groups with the full range of support and preventative services they require.

Labour: reducing child poverty and increasing opportunities for children

A theme of the Labour project, when in power from 1997 to 2010, was to reduce child poverty and increase opportunities for children and young people, particularly those from poorer backgrounds (Hills,

2009). There were a number of interconnected policy initiatives and themes, although it is beyond the scope of this chapter to deal with them fully. These included a focus on 'education, the care and well-being of children, financial support for families with children, services for families, parental employment, work/family reconciliation and family functioning' (Daly, 2010, p. 433). Garret (2009) suggests the initiatives could be encompassed by focusing on 'social exclusion' and measures that saw paid work as a route out of poverty and towards 'social inclusion'.

Labour overhauled the benefits system to 'make work pay', which had some measure of success as a route out of poverty (Brewer and Shephard, 2004). It also introduced measures to tackle social exclusion through education (Penn, 2007); expanded childcare provision to assist parents into work; and encouraged health and social care services to meet children's needs at an earlier stage (Daly, 2010). While Lister (2004) argues that Labour's policies, taken as a whole, represented a new paradigm in childcare, Daly's (2010, p. 442) analysis suggests that, although Labour brought about some changes to family policy, a market-oriented model remained. Without a significant policy paradigm shift, subsequent more market-oriented Coalition policies could readily be implemented, as they represented some level of continuity. Of all Labour's initiatives, it was Sure Start which brought the various themes together into an EI policy.

Sure Start and targeted intervention

The Sure Start programme, established in 1998, was seen as key to Labour's policy commitment to eradicate child poverty by 2020. Glass, the civil servant behind its creation, describes it as being:

> targeted at children under four and their families in areas of need. It is part of the government's policy to prevent social exclusion and aims to improve the life chances of younger children through better access to early education and play, health services for children and parents, family support and advice on nurturing (Glass, 1999, p. 257).

The programme was limited to specified areas initially, to 'ensure that those in the greatest need will benefit most' (Glass, 1999, p. 257).

The policy was aimed at families who lived in poor areas – although Glass did not use the words 'poor' or 'poverty', preferring 'need' – as he believed that the early years of a child's life were crucial as it was then that the child was highly susceptible to external, environmental influences. Thus, high levels of disadvantage in early childhood would increase the risk of exclusion in later life (ibid., p. 261). The policy was intended to connect with several other anti-poverty strategies, outlined at its launch in 1998, by Gordon Brown and David Blunkett:

> Children living in poverty is one of the biggest challenges facing our country and one of the biggest problems that this government aims to tackle. Sure Start is an investment – not only in better services but in our children. Sure Start will help level the playing field for children in disadvantaged areas. … Sure Start aims to provide pathways out of poverty through practical support and advice (*Local Government Chronicle*, 1999).

From an initial 250 projects with diverse aims and targets, Sure Start expanded to 550. With the adoption in 2004 of *Every Child Matters* (DES, 2003) Sure Start was rolled out and upgraded, leading Glass (2005) to question how much of its founding community-based principles had been abandoned in the move to local authority control and to an emphasis on getting mothers back to work. The 'upgrade' to embrace 800,000 children was announced in 2006 (*Local Government Chronicle*, 2006), and Eisenstadt (2011) saw the expansion as a welcome shift towards universalism, suggesting that this was the government's intention, as targeted programmes could not meet the needs of all families. This was supported by strong European evidence suggesting that improvements to childcare and reducing child poverty could be made only through the provision of universal services (Lorenz, 2006; Freitag and Vatter, 2009).

Sure Start's effectiveness has been subject to debate (see Eisenstadt, 2011), yet it placed the question of supporting families in children's early years on the political agenda and linked this to poverty and disadvantage. It suggested that, to address social exclusion and to increase social justice, there needed to be a series of policy interventions addressing social inequality. Many Sure Start projects, however, had focused on parenting skills, in what appears to be a targeting of poor families and their child-rearing practices – a continuation of regulatory social service interventions (Jones and Novak, 1993; Garrett, 2009) – although it was also a method of improving social networks and of developing social capital (Price and Simpson, 2007).

Labour's commitment to abolishing child poverty proved difficult to sustain. Even in the early years of the pledge, critics thought the government unlikely to meet the target without addressing growing levels of income inequality (Hills *et al.*, 2009). The measurement – 60% of median income – was a standard relative poverty measure, accepted by the Child Poverty Action Group (CPAG). Thus, 'absolute' increases in the incomes of low earners would make the target more difficult to reach, if higher incomes increased at a faster rate. In the context of social justice, the pledge to abolish child poverty, alongside other measures to improve the experiences of children and families, was highly significant. It cemented the link between people's (including children's) experiences and structural factors, and it removed poverty from the realm of lifestyle choice, as argued by neo-liberal commentators (Murray, 1990).

Sure Start, poverty and work

A policy objective of the Blair governments (1997–2005) was the abolition of child poverty by 2020. Early intervention and parenting programmes were intended to address this in two ways. First, by ensuring that children received high-quality care through improving parenting skills, in the hope that this in itself would impact on children's life chances (NESST, 2010, p. 22).

Second, by encouraging parents, mainly single mothers, into work.

> Were we trying to ameliorate the effect of poverty on children or make children less poor? Ameliorating the effect is what we do on parent-support and high-quality children's programmes, but the only way to make children less poor is through employment. Those two go hand-in-hand. The reduction of child poverty must be at the forefront of the thinking of children's centre leaders and practitioners. The element of the core offer relating to the services of Jobcentre

Plus would, in our view, be more effectively expressed as a commitment to support families' economic well-being. This would encompass not only Jobcentre Plus input but also skills and training opportunities, and a range of advice aimed at helping families achieve financial independence (NESST, 2010, p. 23).

Thus, the economic agenda was laid bare. While addressing child poverty through parental paid work may have been a valid policy objective, it reveals an underlying economic agenda which began to emerge around early years provision, and was underscored by other policy developments relating to work and benefits – a continuous feature of Labour policy (Daly, 2010).

The Common Assessment Framework: Early Intervention for 'problem' families

Sure Start targeted early years parenting interventions, but Labour also introduced measures designed to meet a wider range of children's needs, including those of older children, at an earlier stage (Garret, 2009; Daly, 2010). Twin components of 'prevention' – a common and recurring theme in the social work literature (see for example, Hardiker *et al.*, 1991; Sinclair *et al.*, 1997; Morris, 2012) – and financial arguments that EI would save money through prevention (Glass, 1999) underpinned the concept of lower-level assessments and interventions inherent in the Common Assessment Framework (CAF). It connected with the five elements of *Every Child Matters* (DES, 2003), implemented following the review into the death of Victoria Climbié.

The intention of the CAF was twofold. First, it ensured a basic assessment of needs was undertaken on all children who were thought of as being 'in need' (as defined by the Children Act 1989, s.17). Second, it was intended to be a multi-professional assessment, and often the teams included a range of professional groups and support staff. By bringing professionals together the combined aim was to cement a low threshold level of support at an early stage in the identification of potentially problem families. This was augmented by the broader concept of 'safeguarding', in contrast to the more targeted interventions associated with 'child protection' (Carpenter *et al.*, 2007).

The CAF enabled early assessment, intervention and a flexible level of support, although different threshold criteria were applied in local arrangements to manage demand (Garrett, 2009). The CAF, like Sure Start, became a mechanism for the identification of risk, often resulting in higher levels of child protection referrals (Tunstill and Allnock, 2007), possibly as a consequence of higher levels of surveillance. Questions of surveillance and control are a continuing feature of policy analyses, and Garret (2009) argues that this was the underlying feature of Labour's childcare policies.

Surveillance and control have always been an inherent feature of social work practice (Price and Simpson, 2007), while a consequence – intended or unintended – of higher levels of support and intervention is more professional input, more support services, inevitably resulting in greater visibility for families who were experiencing difficulties (see Garrett, 2009). Support and EI did not replace child protection services, even though the term was dropped and replaced with the arguably more benign notion of 'safeguarding' in the Children Act 2004, and a bifurcate policy was followed (Hayes and Spratt, 2014). Nonetheless, during the first ten years of the twenty-first century, significant moves towards a more integrated system of EI and support, including – but not restricted to – early years, had been established in England.

The Coalition: Policy continuity?

The Coalition inherited a well-established set of EI policies, in relation to early years and also the early identification of potential family difficulties. The Coalition also had to cope with an economy that was in danger of falling into deficit as a result of bailing out the banks after the economic crash of 2008. This is an important consideration since 'austerity' became a byword for the Coalition as it sought to create a political narrative that this was a consequence of Labour's profligacy, as opposed to an all-party agreement; this debate continued throughout the Coalition's term of office (Richards, 2011).

There were changes to the nature of EI projects and their organisation. Allen (2011) reiterates an earlier argument that the management of early years projects be managed outside the public sector. The Coalition embraced this recommendation, and in 2013 the Early Intervention Foundation, a charitable organisation, was established. Its role was to be one of coordination and to work in partnership with other non-governmental organisation (NGOs) and local authorities to promote a range of EIs.

Using Salford and Birmingham city councils as two different examples of EI policy, the extent of local variations can be seen. In 2015, Salford set out its aim, which appears to be a clear continuation of existing provision and policy:

> ... to work in partnership to improve outcomes for children, young people and families. The aim is to address problems at the earliest opportunity before they are able to escalate and by helping to break the longer-term intergenerational cycle of poor outcomes. Early intervention requires a shift in focus on to the causes rather than the symptoms of problems, with investment in early intervention, which has been proven to reduce the demand on specialist services in the longer term (Salford City Council, 2015).

Birmingham is a local authority facing particular financial pressures, with its leader, Sir Albert Bore, in an interview for *The Guardian*, estimating that it faces a 'ticking timebomb of financial cuts' (Butler, 2014). The city council, the largest in England, has come under close scrutiny since Labour regained control from a Conservative–Liberal Democrat coalition in 2012. Bore estimates that the council will need to make cuts of more than £800 million in the three years from 2015, effectively losing 60% of its controllable budget. He argues that a consequence will be that it will be unable to fulfil many of its traditional roles (ibid.). Accordingly, Birmingham City Council is using the latest government legislation to undertake a full review of all the services it provides, including EI:

> This Review sets out to examine how early years services produce improved outcomes for children and their families, and will focus on the following areas:

- researching cost-effective good-quality early interventions;
- mapping the current services available;
- listening to what children, parents and local people value about Early Years Services;
- looking for the best we can afford (Birmingham City Council, 2014).

It could be argued that there is nothing particularly controversial about the review's remit, but in the economic context of the level of reductions in expenditure facing the city council it is noteworthy that two of the four areas are explicitly concerned with the economic impact.

Meanwhile, Salford City Council's aims, by contrast, may have an underlying theme of value for money, but this is inferred only from the idea that EI will save money in the longer term.

Despite some closures of many of the original Sure Start programmes nationally, other local family centres and the demise of universal provision, the concept of EI appears to be in good health at least intellectually and as a policy aim. It remains a feature of local authority provision, albeit under threat of diminishing and/or being transferred to the private sector.

The Coalition has continued the policy emphasis towards earlier interventions later in a child's life or to support and intervene in families with older children, notably in relation to risk and possible child protection. This had begun with the CAF and gained renewed impetus with the cautious adoption of the Munro report (Munro, 2011). This saw the beginning of a shift in the way local authorities provided services to families, who were to be assessed as either 'in need' (s.17) or 'at risk' (s.47) in relation to the Children Act 1989. Munro's report was based on the so-called 'Hackney model', which was premised on EI and accurate assessments, bringing together a range of professionals, including child psychologists, in relatively small, community- or locality-based teams headed by a consultant social worker. The model, also called 'Reclaiming Social Work', drew wide support in the social work profession, as the main thrust of Munro's argument was to move social work away from managerialism, towards its roots as a person-focused profession. The initial evaluation of the model outlined a more person-focused service, and a service that would reduce costs (Cross, *et al.*, 2010), an apparent 'win–win' situation for increasingly hard-pressed local authorities. Thus, there is another shift in the way 'things are done' and services delivered.

In 2011, the prime minister (David Cameron) announced the Troubled Families programme (Cameron, 2011). His speech, a few months after riots in a number of English cities in summer 2011, concluded with a commitment of '£448 million to turning around the lives of 120,000 Troubled Families by the end of this Parliament' and the appointment of Louise Casey to head up the initiative. This was not merely an organisational change, since a feature was not only shifting responsibility away from local authorities to the NGO sector but also moving it away from qualified professionals to volunteers or people with lower-level qualifications. Casey, in her speech to the Local Government Association's annual conference in 2013, suggested that part of the problem faced by such families was the collusion of social workers (Wheeler, 2013).

In summary, the Coalition has remained committed to the notion of EI, and this can be viewed as a policy continuation. There have been significant shifts towards the NGO sector as part of the Coalition's wider assault on local authorities and some aspects of social work (see below). Whereas Labour combined EI policies with a commitment to end child poverty, the Coalition moved away from this pledge and in doing so created a policy language that sought to characterise the poor as being feckless (Jones, 2011; McKenzie, 2015).

The coalition and (child) poverty

Labour's measure of relative poverty (including child poverty) could be reached only by measures that sought to raise the level of income of the poorest and also to limit the incomes of the very richest (Hills *et al.*, 2009). Labour's focus was on incomes, augmented by a range of measures, including tax credits, targeted at the working poor. Data from the CPAG (2014) indicates that of the 3.5 million children living in poverty (around 25% of all children), two-thirds of these are in households where at least one family member works.

Coalition measures in successive budgets since 2010 to limit benefit payments under the guise of fairness has worsened the situation. The so-called bedroom tax has impacted adversely on many families, especially those with disabled children, who were already more likely to be poor (Duffy, 2014). The CPAG further estimates that it was a combination of lone parents working and increases in the levels of benefits paid to families with children that were key factors in Labour lifting more than one million children out of child poverty between 1998 and 2011. It argues that there is now an upwards trend, which will result in more than 4.7 million children living in poverty by 2020. Thus, increasing employment levels began under Labour, but the Coalition have refocused the debate to suggest that it is solely lack of work that causes and maintains poverty. They have abandoned Labour's target to abolish child poverty by 2020, and the argument that poverty is not just to do with money has been at the heart of an emerging discourse about poverty and EI (Duncan Smith and Osborne, 2014; see also below).

Early Adoption and the Children and Families Act 2014

Aspects of neuroscience research have become fashionable within government policy circles but are not without their critics (Featherstone *et al.*, 2014). In opposition, Iain Duncan Smith had welcomed Graham Allen's initial report into EI in 2009; and his subsequent report *Early Intervention: The Next Steps* (Allen, 2011) was promoted as Coalition policy. Its second chapter focuses on a developing body of research in neuroscience, which examines brain development and suggests that lasting damage could be done to children through parental neglect in their very early years of development. These debates are themselves controversial both in their findings (Breuer, 1999) and in the application of such findings (Wastel and White, 2012). Wastel and White's (2012) paper is a much-needed corrective to the arguments of some neuroscientists which were outlined in the Allen (2011) report. This debate has been continued by Pithouse and Emlyn Jones in Chapter 1 (above) of *Early Intervention: Supporting and Strengthening Families*. The significance lies, however, in how these claims have influenced aspects of EI policies.

As early as 2009, Sir Martin Narey had argued:

> More babies should be removed from their mothers at birth
> before irreparable harm is inflicted. There is an argument
> to be made ... that even intervening at this early stage is too
> late (Walsh, 2010, p. 12).

Such thinking has underpinned the Children and Families Act 2014 and policy changes in adoption practice. The Children and Family Court Advisory and Support Service (CAFCASS) Plus scheme, piloted in Coventry and Warwickshire, was developed with the aim of reducing the length of time taken by care proceedings, which had reached seventy weeks in 2010 (Broadhurst *et al.*, 2013). This was to be achieved through greater collaboration and a pre-proceedings approach, often resulting in greater use of placements within the child's extended family (kinship care placements). This is one of a range of developments and initiatives to speed up care proceedings, which was precipitated by an announcement by Prime Minister David Cameron in 2012. He argued that the adoption process needed to become fairer and faster, describing the policy of same-race placements as 'absurd barriers' – though there appeared to be little evidence for the statement (Malik, 2012).

While these measures provided a very clear set of policy directions, which local authorities and others began to use and refer to, they were also linked to greater flexibility in the system to allow (even encourage) foster-carers to become adopters. Perhaps as a consequence, the number of children placed for adoption in 2012/13 was the highest ever, at 3,980 – a 20% increase from 2009 (DES, 2013)

This chapter has sketched the Coalition's policies in relation to early years interventions, EI in problem families and the move to earlier, more authoritative legal intervention with the result of an increased use of adoption. There have been aspects of continuity from Labour, as well as some policy shifts. The remainder of the chapter will seek to explore the underlying assault on the poor and on state agencies, which have characteristically sought to provide services. It is through such an analysis that the changes in emphasis to early years policies by the Coalition can be reviewed and understood as part of a wider policy narrative.

Targeting the poor

A feature of Allen's (2011) report is how families who need support are characterised by drug and/or alcohol misuse, crime, domestic and other violence and that they show poor bonding, social isolation, negative behaviour management, poor parenting skills, postnatal depression and lack of stimulation for the child (Allen, 2011, pp. 15–16). Allen draws on a range of evidence and then suggests EI aims for children to be 'life ready', that is:

> having the social and emotional capability to enter the labour market; understanding the importance and the social, health and emotional benefits of entering work, the impacts of drug and alcohol misuse, crime and domestic and other violence (Allen, 2011, p. 9).

Allen, a Labour MP who represents one of Nottingham's most deprived areas, makes no concessions to the possibility that such difficulties may be the consequences of poverty, as opposed to the causes of poverty. This tension has been played out within social work and social welfare for more than 150 years and has generated considerable debate (Price and Simpson, 2007). Yet personal characteristics are a recurring theme throughout Allen's (2011) report and also in Field's (2010) report, in which he suggests income transfers alone will not reduce poverty. These two reports run the risk of being used to demonise the poor, even though this would not have been their intention.

Allen's (2011) report cannot be dismissed in its entirety, as it highlights some positive developments taken on by other countries in the UK, which are outlined in other chapters in this book. However, one of its uses in England has unfortunately been to target a particular group – the poor.

Before considering the current debates around austerity and its impact on EI, this chapter has argued that a parallel set of aims has emerged. A financial report on the Troubled Families programme (Communities and Local Government, 2012) refers to the family types that need intervention. These include those with: emotional and mental health problems; drug and alcohol misuse; long-term health conditions; and health problems caused by domestic abuse alongside 'under eighteen conceptions'. This characterises 'poor families' as beset by a range of 'personal' failings, which are to be addressed through a range of early interventions. This focus on poor people's failings lead Featherstone *et al.* (2014) to suggest that it creates an inhumane and punitive form of social work. Yet, the Government suggests that a failure to intervene will compound potential disadvantage and ultimately cost the exchequer more money – a recurring justification of the high-profile scheme.

Austerity and early Intervention

This chapter has set out the Coalition approach to EI and has noted the shift towards an increased focus on individual responsibility and away from more structural measures to address aspects of poverty and the attendant consequences of low incomes. Simpson and Connor (2011, p. 4) argue that those who provide welfare services need to become policy literate, to understand that policies are 'particular prescriptions from a range of options available'. In this context, the Coalition has recast poverty not as something that could affect anyone but as a set of personal failings. This is exemplified by Cameron (2011) in his policy to develop stronger families:

> Strong families are the foundation of a bigger, stronger society. This is not some romanticised fiction. It is a fact. There's a whole body of evidence that shows how a bad relationship between parents means a child is more likely to live in poverty, fail at school, end up in prison or be unemployed in later life (Cameron, 2011).

Money, or rather the lack of it, becomes largely ignored, however. Cooper and Stewart (2013) reviewed the research evidence around many of the Coalition's themes outlined here and found that, out of thirty-four studies, in only five of them had money not affected the outcomes for children. Their paper concludes that increases in income will have a considerably greater impact on families at the lower end of the income scale (Cooper and Stewart, 2013, p. 54). Earlier studies (Cunha and Heckman, 2007; 2008, in Cooper and Stewart, 2013, pp. 54, 61) show that income is of considerable importance during the child's early years. There is, therefore, a body of evidence running counter to the government's policy focus in early years provision. Cooper and Stewart conclude:

> Our review indicates clearly that money makes a difference to children's outcomes. Poorer children have worse cognitive, social-behavioural and health outcomes in part *because they are poorer*, and not just because poverty is correlated with other household and parental characteristics. The evidence relating to cognitive development and school achievement is the clearest and there is the most of it, followed by that on social and behavioural development (Cooper and Stewart, 2013, p. 5).

In a recent review, Lupton *et al.* (2105) demonstrate how, since 2012 when Labour's earlier welfare measures were ended by the Coalition, austerity measures have had a disproportionately adverse impact on the poor. Specifically in relation to EI, they note that, while there is more access to education than in 2010 for children from 'disadvantaged households', reductions in child benefit and the abolition of baby-tax credit have resulted in a 26% decline in funding per child. Furthermore, there are fewer Sure Start places available, and families may need to travel further to access the services (ibid., p. 46). The targeting of Sure Start to families 'at risk of poor outcomes' (see above) has meant that it is unlikely that families will receive support unless they have been assessed to fall within this group (ibid., p. 17), as Sure Start expenditure fell by 32% since 2010 as a consequence of Coalition austerity measures (ibid., p. 22). Lupton *et al.* (2015) suggest that service delivery has held up well in the face of cuts, mainly because staff work harder and there is a greater reliance on volunteers, even though there have been 622 closures of Sure Start centres, since the Coalition took office (Lupton *et al.*, 2015, p. 44). In their review of the Coalition's benefit spending Hood and Phillips (2015) demonstrate that, as a consequence of specific policy changes, spending on working-age adults and children has been reduced by £7 billion, through a realignment of welfare expenditure in favour of increased state pensions. Thus, austerity measures have disproportionately impacted on the poor through cuts in services. Despite extensive rhetoric about reducing welfare expenditure, actual reductions were minimal (3%), leading to the possible conclusion that money has been redistributed from the poor to the better off (Toynbee, 2015).

Conclusion

The Coalition has continued many of Labour's EI policies but has arguably taken the project of 'active citizenship' within a neo-liberal context to punitive levels. While Labour might be accused of establishing a framework within which this could happen, their policies ran alongside wider fiscal measures aimed at reducing income inequality. These measures, under the guise of austerity, have been discarded by the Coalition. The abandonment of any attempt to address income inequality has led to increased attention being paid to families who are poor and deemed to be failing, compounded by a demonising of the poor. Developments towards early adoptions, premised on some of the research used to promote EI strategies, are another recent feature.

The chapter has offered a political and policy account of EI in England and has attempted to unravel a series of policy trajectories. Pockets of good practice in EI certainly exist, and some are outlined in later chapters of this book, but they possibly exist in spite of and not because of the Coalition's policies. Early intervention and family support have many positives and variations as other contributions in this book illustrate, but the Coalition policies in England are arguably failing to support some of the children and families in greatest need.

CHAPTER 4

Family Support and child welfare in Ireland: Capacities and possibilities

Pat Dolan, Berni Smith, Mary Smith and John Davis

Introduction

The processes by which vulnerable children and youth can be best supported and protected remains a challenge for governments, policymakers, service managers, frontline workers and families and communities alike. Despite much rhetoric in recent years, this remains an issue in many countries including the Republic of Ireland. Ten years ago having been a wealthy EU member state, Ireland moved swiftly from 'boom to bust' and four years into a major recession it is only now that the implications of this downfall are being fully understood. The huge pressures of austerity, disadvantage, poverty and unemployment on families and communities have run concurrent with a crisis in confidence in relation to the Irish child protection and welfare services system. Reports have specifically highlighted serious failings to protect children from abuse, and there is now a new recognition of the nature and extent of past institutional abuse of children in the care system in Ireland. This, in part, has led to a complete reorganisation of management systems in child protection and welfare and the creation of an entity entitled TUSLA the Child and Family Agency.

This chapter considers both the impact of the recession and the increased recognition of child protection issues within the Irish experience and context. It particularly focuses on matters relating to family support as a process for assisting and sustaining children and families who experience adversity. The chapter is informed by research, policy reports and legislation and connects this recent literature to Irish family support workers' testimonial evidence from an ongoing study being led by the authors. It highlights three common practice considerations: listening to and acting on the voice of the child; the importance of face-to-face direct work; and the usage of a strengths-based perspective in working with children and parents under stress.

Prevention and Early Intervention – Models of Family Support in an Irish Context

In Ireland, since the early 1980s the role and rates of success that accrue from social worker interventions (in particular) have been increasingly challenged by many within and outside of the profession. Since 2009 alone, notable high-profile child protection failures such as the Roscommon incest case (Gibbons, 2010) has instigated strong questioning regarding the efficacy of the social work profession in particular. Social workers, as well as related professionals including teachers and public health visitors, have been questioned (perhaps at times unfairly) on their effective capacity to protect children from harm, and on their ability to offer real assistance and support. This has occurred in the context of a major scandal in respect of the past abuse of children within Irish institutions including orphanages and industrial schools (Ryan, 2009).

In a review of a number of high-profile, state-commissioned inquiry reports, Buckley and O'Nolan (2013) identify repeated unimplemented recommendations, such as information-sharing barriers, absent family support orientation, no culture of listening to children and, overall, insufficient inter-agency collaboration. As part of their review they call for a 'reframing' towards family support preventive practices that would enable professionals to refocus on developing interventions in partnership with children and families. This complements risk-inclusive approaches advocated by Dolan *et al.* (2011). One could argue that this focus has been all but lost to the belief (regardless of its validity) that child welfare in Ireland is now solely about safeguarding children. However, as will be highlighted later, the introduction of the new Child and Family Agency offers new hope and brings together key child-welfare professionals into one organisational structure and highlights family support and its functions as a key part of its work.

In Ireland, the term 'family support' is more traditionally and widely used than in England to describe prevention and EIs to help children and families, both within their own communities as well as in leaving care contexts (Devaney and Dolan, 2014; Frost and Dolan, 2012). In neighbouring Scotland, the term and role has more recently emerged to explain key worker roles in integrated service assessment, design and delivery (Davis and Smith, 2012). This has occurred within a context in Ireland and England in which writers have called for social workers and other professionals to hold the line on their family support functions (Frost and Dolan, 2012), while reviews in England have called for a return to more direct casework and less bureaucratic processes (Munro, 2011). In all three countries, a gap between effective policy and real and direct implementation has been highlighted (Davis and Smith, 2012; Frost and Dolan, 2012). Essentially, the question of identifying practice mechanisms to change the functions of social work practice towards a family-support orientation that includes child protection rather than being a sole function has been seen but not acted on.

The recent establishment in Ireland of TUSLA the Child and Family Agency has joined child welfare professionals (including social workers and social care workers) together in one grouping. The agency advocates for a greater concentration on prevention, early (in the problem) intervention, 'better skills' (fit for purpose) and improved practice (Devaney et al., 2013). This has brought new hope and some expectation for many professionals in child welfare in Ireland. However, new policy alone – no matter how well intentioned – does not necessarily ensure improved practice, and particularly so in a context where a dearth of knowledge has been identified concerning what family support means and how it is understood by professionals and families in the Republic of Ireland (Holt and Dolan, 2010). Similarly, in Scotland it has been argued that a lack of clarity concerning family support has hindered multi-professional working (Davis and Smith, 2012). Thus, in this chapter some 'reminding and reconfiguring' of core factors for social workers and related professionals in supporting children and families living in extreme adversity may be timely in the Irish context and elsewhere.

The Role of Family support Workers

Family support workers now have a number of clearly designated roles: working face to face with children, youth and families in planning, delivering and reviewing interventions; collaborating closely with other professionals, voluntary groups and community members; stimulating and facilitating peer support; and providing out-of-hours, wraparound, practical advice and emotional support (Davis and Smith, 2012). This means that family support professionals work across all tiers of intervention from day-to-day frontline to immediate and acute contexts, while continuously working towards key family support principles such as minimum intervention, strengths-based working, flexible delivery and meeting families' self-identified requirements (Dolan and Brady, 2012). In order to illustrate the work and views of this workforce in an Irish context, fifteen family support workers were chosen at random to participate in a set of one-to-one interviews as part of a research project to gain insight into what they believed to be key in their work with families. Excerpts from their testimonies are utilised later as an additional source of information in respect of key issues for policy and practice in child welfare in Ireland.

The Impact of the Recession on Vulnerable Children and Families

Ireland has moved with speed from being perceived as one of the wealthiest countries in the EU to one in financial crisis needing a bailing out of its banks because the survival of its financial systems was in jeopardy. An increase in children and families drifting into debt and poverty has accompanied this process. Some politicians and economists initially referred to this demise as a 'soft landing' but later and swiftly had to describe the situation as a 'sudden severe crisis'. At the beginning of the millennium, the Irish exchequer was so strong that there was an overheated economy with too much cash in circulation, resulting in citizens being given a state-sponsored cash bonus for participation in a national saving scheme. Post the economic collapse and in complete contradiction to this, many Irish families are now confronted by severe cuts in basic health and education services, an inability to pay mortgages and the consequences of unemployment, such as householders moving towards homelessness.

While the exact scale and impact of the recession on children, parents and families is unknown, two important recent research reports are indicative of the problem. That by the Economic Social Research Institute has indicated that almost a third of children have been deprived of essentials, such as food or clothing, during the recent recession (McGinnity *et al.*, 2014). Similarly, research analysis by Johnston (2013) at the National Social and Economic Council has focused on the very basic and tangible issue of jobless households in Ireland in the light of the recession. Johnston's analysis suggests not only that Ireland is experiencing a higher rate than other countries of jobless households with accompanying adversity, but also the link to hidden poverty is highlighted. Both reports demonstrate the new hardship on children and families resulting from the Irish recession as well as remind us that this occurs in a context where services that were already stretched in terms of capacity to meet need will in all likelihood experience further pressure.

Given this now-understandable strain on child and family services, a move towards ensuring value for money has focused on tangible results accruing from interventions, and this is not unique to Ireland with 'better outcomes' now being seen as part of our common language. There has also been a strong push towards proven or 'promising' interventions such as robustly evaluated, 'manualised' programmes: for example, youth mentoring (Dolan *et al.*, 2011) and innovative school and community-based projects (Coen *et al.*, 2012). In part, this push for 'evidence strong' interventions has developed from the major Atlantic philanthropies/Irish government-funded programme which over the last fifteen years has funded prevention and EI family support initiatives. However, important as outcomes are, the need to ensure children, youth and families can cope in terms of 'getting by' has also been highlighted (Pinkerton and Dolan, 2007). In particular, given the recent Irish history of recession, the value placed on the importance of coping with adversity over time may now deserve greater emphasis.

Three Core Practice Considerations

This chapter has considered child safeguarding failures and subsequent inquiries; legislative and policy developments; and Ireland's emphasis on Family Support. It will now consider three core practice factors. While these are not exclusive to other issues, it is the view of the authors that these three components are particularly noteworthy in the context of family support and the ten family support principles developed for the Irish government (Dolan *et al.*, 2011).

Direct work

The importance of Irish social workers (in particular) as well as other professionals holding on to their direct work role in supporting children and families has been well highlighted in Ireland (Dolan *et al.*, 2011; Frost and Dolan, 2012). Recent research has posed questions concerning the extent to which children's services professionals are involved in regular direct work with families (Davis, 2011). It is argued that some professionals are restricted by rigid systems, hierarchical management and over-bureaucratic working and that this inflexibility prevents them from being available to work directly with children. One of the advantages of the emergence of the family support worker role is that the professional can act as a key contact located near to families who can respond in a variety of roles of direct support (Davis and Smith, 2012). The worker's role involves building trust, recognising historical issues, acknowledging family context and supporting the capacity of families to articulate solutions to their life problems. Solutions may require redistribution of emotional, financial and or legal resources, and families indicate that strong relationships are built with professionals when staff are perceived as responding quickly to issues that arise, interact in non-judgemental ways and adopt socially just practices. Direct work with children, youth and parents enables families to witness this in action and first hand.

Certainly in recent years there has been a noticeable waning of direct face-to-face casework by social workers, and in many instances they, as well as others, regret this change. It could be argued that many social workers entered the profession to do individualised supportive and enabling actions with children and families, but find that over time their role is further and further removed from direct face-to-face working. In some ways, their role may be more of a case manager who directs an 'orchestra of interventions' rather than who plays any 'lead instruments'. This move away from direct work was particularly highlighted as a failing in the Roscommon incest case inquiry (Gibbons, 2010) where direct work with children and parents in the home was seen as purely the work of others and not a task for social workers. What is encouraged from the learning in this case is the need for social workers to return to more direct face-to-face work with children and parents rather than standing back relying on the testimony of other professionals to gauge success.

The importance of direct working has been recognised not just in the UK by Munro (2011) but also in the USA by Brooks-Gunn *et al.* (2012), who have stated strongly that direct face-to-face work with parents can help reduce child maltreatment. What is somewhat disconcerting is that this message is not new for Ireland, the UK or the USA. In the early 1980s, in the Jasmine Beckford tragedy in the UK, social workers and health visitors were seen as negligent in not doing enough direct work as part of a method of safeguarding, and similarly in the mid-1990s in the death of Kelly Fitzgerald in Ireland (Western Health Board, 1996) direct work was not seen as being utilised well enough as a method of detection or protection. More recently, our current study with family support workers (alluded to earlier) attests strongly to ways direct work with parents can enable better protection of children.

A recurring theme throughout the interviews with Irish family support workers was the need to build a trusting relationship with the families before the 'real' work could commence. Workers agreed that this process requires time, consistency and being available to the families. Worker A stressed the importance of time. She said: 'The whole idea is that we have time, we don't just fly in and out.' She pointed out that the time is spent: 'getting to know the family, building up a good positive rapport, gaining trust with the family'. Worker B spoke about 'putting in the hours with the family' and how this led to individuals becoming familiar and at ease with their key worker. 'You're going into their houses so much that they think you're part of the furniture', she said. 'We really get in there.' Finally, Worker C said: 'You have to take the time to gain a person's confidence and then other things might start coming out.' Finally, another respondent commenting on how families perceive the service stated: 'They start to see that I can be approached, we're a 24/7 service so there's always someone at the end of a phone if we're needed.'

The voices of children and young people

There has been a recent paradigm in Ireland towards hearing the voice of the child in more real ways, particularly at a policy level. For example, through the creation of Dáil na nÓg (Ireland's children and youth parliament), as well as the office of the Ombudsman for Children, young people have been given opportunities to share their views on matters such as the school systems, bullying and peer pressures, and youth suicide. However, while this is evident at a policy level, at the harder, individualised, level-of-life experiences and in cases of serious failings to protect young people their voices were either unheard, not listened to and/or not acted on. For example, in the Roscommon incest case the report of inquiry found that the views of children on their hardship and abuse by their parents was unheard by professionals working with them (Gibbons, 2010). As Davis and Smith (2012) point out, if participation of young people on matters of their own welfare is to be taken seriously it goes much further than hearing what they have to say. It requires actions on the part of all concerned.

Professionals in the Irish child welfare system are probably continuing to get better at listening to what young people have to say, and there is also improved engagement on the part of government and services. For example, a study in 2010 of Young Carers actively sought out and heard testimonies from children and youth carers for family members including, in some cases, parents with a disability (Kennan *et al.*, 2012). Young Carers spoke of their need to have their own time and experiences and how being a Young Carer impeded their education opportunities. This research, which was commissioned by the Department of Children and Youth Affairs, led to the creation of a family support programme specially designed to help children and young people caring for family members.

This need for professionals to listen closely to those they work with was also voiced strongly by family support workers in our current research project. Workers emphasised the importance of listening to what the children had to say about their situation. One worker reflected:

> When you start working with a family first it can seem very chaotic, everyone vying for attention but when they realise that you are there for all of them [the family] and are

willing to listen, things settle down; you notice it most with the children.

Worker F said: 'It's as though no one has ever asked the children what they think. They seem surprised that you're interested.' Similarly, worker D noted that listening to the children can help to inform the work with parents:

It can surprise you how much they [the children] under-stand about their situation. When you get down to it, they don't look for big things, they usually only want to be seen and given practical help.

Taking a strengths-based perspective

Strengths-based approaches require a shift in services to a position where the different actors involved become willing to learn from each other (Saleeby, 2004). Such approaches have been defined as recognising that children, young people, parents, professionals, rela-tives and various community members possess their own kinds of expertise that can form the basis for minimum intervention and maximum collaborative problem-solving (Dolan, 2006). They are contrasted with deficit models of interventions that involve adult professionals assuming they know best, promoting normative thinking, dominating children's spaces, seeking to intervene uni-formly in communities, ignoring diversity and requiring children and parents to conform to existing service structures (Davis and Smith, 2012). This theoretical shift has sought to connect and make available to professionals ideas on social support, resilience, social ecology, social justice and social capital (Dolan, 2006). Part of this philosophy and approach encourages professionals, service manag-ers and families themselves to build on the strengths and resources they can muster. At the same time as this strengths-based approach emerged, the family support worker role was embedded into Irish social policy at government level and through *The Agenda for Chil-dren's Services* practices and support materials were developed to promote innovative ways of involving families in resolving their own problems (Office of the Minister for Children, 2004). Family welfare conferencing, which has been used in Ireland since the early 1990s, best typifies this approach and encourages a strengths-based perspective to solutions even in cases of abuse (Morris and Connolly, 2012).

While it may seem obvious that, by adopting a strengths-based perspective, workers take the chance of missing risk in child protection cases, it has also been well argued that recognising strengths as well as deficits is key in order to build resilience in children, youth and families (Luthar and Zelazo, (2003). This is not to suggest that, where harm occurs, it should be demoted in terms of importance or urgency, but rather that, in order for long-term solutions to be sustained, strengths have to be identified and made effective in families including among members who fail in their duties to children and young people.

A strengths-based perspective can also be seen as useful by policymakers in terms of an efficient use of resources. This approach essentially allows services to access existing resources within the family and community and to nurture social and human capital. In the Irish context, having regular access to families in their own home environment gives family support workers an insight into the unique and multiple strengths of differing family members. Importantly, it opens up workers' ability to analyse context and to observe small positive changes that might otherwise be missed. Worker C spoke about a family that had been referred due to concerns about the parent's capacity to organise routines, due to a learning disability. The worker noted that one of the children received her prescribed medication very sporadically at the start of the intervention. Within weeks, with regular and consistent guidance by an extended family member, a routine had been established and lapses became increasingly rare. This indicated to the worker that, with support, this parent was capable of implementing routines, and she began working with the parent and children to establish clear childcare and household management routines in the home. Worker C also spoke about 'instilling hope' and 'inspiring confidence' and commented that these small steps had become a powerful catalyst leading to significant positive changes in other aspects of the children's care. Similarly, Worker B saw her role as 'empowering them to look for the help themselves next time as well as seeing if they could sort matters without having to turn to a professional'.

Conclusion

The prospect of investing in the human capital of families where longstanding issues of social exclusion and parenting difficulties produces significant savings to a range of services can bring important benefits to families themselves. Evaluations of intensive family support projects have shown the range of benefits and outcomes are clearly positive in the majority of cases (Batty and Flint, 2013). We would suggest that promoting the social and human capital of some of the vulnerable and complex families should be a key investment not avoided; instead it should be seen as part of a 'family support building block'. Similarly, social workers and other professionals should revisit and embrace the fact that successful working with children and families is based on real and robust relationships between professionals and those they work with and for, and this should be retained as essential policy and practice.

The triad of practices identified and discussed here including direct work, giving voice and strengths-based working could provide a timely focus and refocus for policymakers and practitioners alike. The lessons from the Irish context shared here in all likelihood are not that unusual and have currency in other countries but, yet again, they highlight that good policy alone does not ensure good practice. But what is probably unique to Ireland is our realisation that, in the light of a current recovering economy with many families under strain and those working with them feeling the pressure, the need to provide effective instrumental and emotional family support will not go away and deserves to be valued.

CHAPTER 5

Family group conferencing: A promising practice in the context of early intervention in Northern Ireland

David Hayes, Michael Hoy and Paul Kellagher

Introduction

This chapter discusses family group conferencing (FGC) as a promising practice in the context of EI in Northern Ireland (NI). It begins by briefly describing the organisational and policy context for the delivery of services to children and families and then moves on to discuss the FGC model and how its use has developed within NI. Two specific examples of the use of FGC within EI initiatives are then outlined: one delivered by a voluntary organisation (Action for Children/AfC); and one by a statutory agency (the Southern Health and Social Care Trust). In the first of these initiatives, FGC is a central component of a wider EI service which is delivered to children and families who require additional support in order to promote social inclusion and reduce levels of vulnerability within the family. In the second initiative, however, which is focused on young people admitted to care, FGC has played a peripheral, although beneficial, role. The chapter concludes by summarising the promising aspects of FGC in terms of the delivery of EI.

The Northern Ireland Context

NI is the smallest of the four constituent countries of the UK with a population of just over 1.8 million people recorded by the UK Census 2011 with 25% of the population comprising children and young people (NISRA, 2014). It is also the youngest part of the UK as the state of NI was created as a result of the campaign for Irish Home Rule. The Government of Ireland Act 1920 divided Ireland into two areas, and the first NI Parliament was established in Belfast in 1921. NI is also one of the most deprived regions of the UK with:

> ... relatively high levels of unemployment disability and poverty ... the lowest wages and one of the lowest labour productivity rates, and it is heavily reliant on the public sector, which is coupled with a weak private sector. These weaknesses reflect a number of unique, interrelated factors, not least the legacy of 30 years of conflict, the demographic structure and the peripheral location ... as well as issues surrounding deprivation and rurality (Ham *et al.*, 2013, pp. 2–3).

In terms of health and social care, NI has had an integrated service delivery system since 1973. The NI Parliament sat until 1972 when, because of continuing and sustained violence and political unrest, direct rule from Westminster was introduced. The arrival of direct rule occurred in parallel to a reorganisation of local government in NI, which saw local councils lose a number of key responsibilities, including those for health and social services, with these being integrated under a new structure of four Health and Social Services Boards operating on a geographical basis (Eastern, Northern, Southern and Western). Devolved government was restored in 1998 to the locally elected NI Assembly established under the terms of the Belfast Agreement of 10 April 1998. The Assembly was, however, suspended in 2002 due to a political crisis; devolved government was restored in 2007 and has been operating continuously since then.

The resumption of devolved government in 2007 coincided with a major reform of public services in NI. The Review of Public Administration (RPA) was 'designed to reduce bureaucracy and administration costs, renew local government and provide greater consistency in the delivery of public services' (Devaney *et al.*, 2010, p. 53). Under the RPA, the overall responsibility for health and social care lies with the Department for Health, Social Services and Public Safety (DHSSPS). The four Health and Social Services Boards have been replaced by a single Health and Social Care Board, which is responsible for commissioning services, managing resources and performance improvement, and five integrated Health and Social Care Trusts (HSCTs) have been established to deliver a mixture of community and hospital-based services on a geographical basis (Belfast, Northern, Southern, South-Eastern and Western).

In relation to the delivery of services to children and families, the policy priorities of the DHSSPS are set out in two key documents: *Care Matters* (DHSSPS, 2007), which focuses on providing support to families in crisis; and *Families Matter* (DHSSPS, 2009a), which deals with improving support and services for all families and children. Both of these documents identify a strategic focus on EI to reduce the need for formal statutory involvement in children and young people's lives by social services. They also complement each other as it is envisaged that the provision of EI and prevention through *Families Matter* will have a positive impact 'on those who might otherwise require higher needs-based intervention' (DHSSPS, 2009a, p. 9). The strategic focus on EI is informed by the NI Family Support Model (adapted from Hardiker *et al.*, 1991), which details four levels of need that can be responded to by four levels of services as outlined in Table 5.1.

The overall aim is to ensure that appropriate services and supports are available to families at the earliest opportunity – either early in the life of the child or at an early stage of difficulties – and at all levels of need.

Table 5.1 The Northern Ireland family support model

Needs	Services
Level 1: All children and young people	Services for the whole population (universal), such as mainstream healthcare, education, leisure facilities
Level 2: Children who are vulnerable	Support for children who are vulnerable, through an assessment of need and targeted through specific services
Level 3: Children in need in the community	Support for families or individual children and young people, where there are chronic or serious problems; these are provided through a complex mix of services across both the statutory and voluntary/community sectors
Level 4: Children in need of rehabilitation	Support for families or individual children and young people, where the family has broken down temporarily or permanently, and where services at levels 1–3 have not met their needs

Family Group Conferencing in Northern Ireland

FGC originated in New Zealand and is strongly influenced by Maori cultural values and based on the traditional Maori *whanau hui* (family meeting) (Hassall, 1996). Since 1989, however, it has been enshrined in New Zealand legislation and is the formal decision-making process for all children for whom decisions or plans need to be made because of care or protection concerns. In these circumstances, it is normally professionals who make plans in consultation with family members, but, in FGC, the child and his or her wider family network comprise the primary planning group while professionals provide information, resources and expertise to the family, facilitating them to develop a plan that addresses the care or protection needs of the child. The plan is developed within the context of 'bottom lines', i.e. clear statements from professionals about what is the absolute minimum requirement to protect the child or young person from harm and the actions that must be taken to address the dangers identified. FGC, therefore, aims to enable families to provide their own solutions to the difficulties they are experiencing and to support partnership working between families and professionals. The FGC process is outlined in Figure 5.1 (Hayes and Houston, 2007, p. 995).

Stage 1: Referral

Stage 2: Preparation

Stage 3: The Conference
a: Information giving
b: Private family time
c: Agreeing the plan

Stage 4: Monitoring

Figure 5.1 The FGC process

An FGC will take place once an initial agreement has been reached between the family and the professionals that decisions and plans should be made for the child or young person concerned. An independent coordinator is then appointed to work with the family to arrange the conference (Stage 1 – Referral). In the preparation phase (Stage 2), the coordinator works with the child or young person and their carers to identify the wider family and supportive networks surrounding the child and contacts them to prepare them for the conference. In the conference itself (Stage 3), the professionals provide the family group with the information they have collected about the child or young person, including a statement of their concerns and the 'bottom line', as well as information about any services or supports that are available. This stage of the conference is chaired by the coordinator. The family members are then invited to draw up a plan for the care or protection of the child using the advice and information provided by the professionals and they undertake this task in private with the professionals withdrawing from the conference. Finally, the family and professionals meet again to agree the plan, discuss any services or support required to implement the plan and decide how it will be monitored and reviewed (Stage 4).

International interest in FGC has been widespread and, in the UK, was initiated when the Family Rights Group hosted some New Zealand practitioners to talk about their experiences (Rickford, 1991). A number of social services departments subsequently established pilot projects, which were reported on in a national evaluation study (Marsh and Crow, 1998) and which influenced the development of FGC in NI. A small number of committed individuals and statutory and voluntary organisations pioneered the use of FGC from the mid-1990s onwards (see Crozier, 2000 and Best and Wilson, 2007 for a detailed account of the evolution of FGC in NI). In 1997, an interest group was formed – the Family Group Conference Forum NI (FGCFNI; www.fgcni.org), which has championed the use of FGC and provided a meeting place for practitioners, managers, policymakers and researchers to support FGC practice and to share learning across the social care, education and criminal justice sectors. A number of FGC projects were established during the late 1990s and early 2000s, and these became firmly established following positive evaluation and research findings (Hayes, 2000a; 2000b; Stephens *et al.*, 2002; Harley, 2005; McCready and Donnelly, 2005).

FGC is currently provided in all five HSCTs in NI and is under-pinned by a set of standards (FGCFNI, 2010) and regional guidance (HSCB, 2011a). The South-Eastern HSCT has delivered an FGC ser-vice within its own area since 1998 and, since 2006, has also delivered FGC to the Belfast HSCT. In-house FGC services have been opera-tional in the Northern HSCT since 2001 and in the Western HSCT since 2005, and in the Southern HSCT a contracted-out FGC service has been provided by Barnardos since 2000. In addition, the Health and Social Care Board commissions a voluntary organisation (AfC) to provide an EI FGC service and this is discussed in the following section.

Action for Children: Early Intervention Family Group Conference Service

AfC's Early Intervention FGC service is part of a broader EI service. It was established in 2009 and, as noted above, is commissioned by the Health and Social Care Board and covers the southern half of the Western HSCT – specifically the local government areas of Fer-managh and Omagh. Its remit is to provide targeted family support services to families and children deemed to be vulnerable, generally at level two of the NI Family Support Model. The service is based on the principle of providing meaningful support to families at an early stage of difficulty, and helping them before these difficulties become compounded over time. Family support and EI practice also involves working with wider family members and other people from the community as central players and FGC is an approach that ena-bles the positive enlistment of support from family and other infor-mal sources of help (Marsh and Crow, 1998; O'Brien, 2000).

The AfC Early Intervention FGC service is provided by a mixed team of social workers, family support practitioners and an FGC coordinator. Referrals to the coordinator are provided both inter-nally from the wider EI service team and externally from professional and families themselves. Much of the use of FGC in NI has focused on the child protection and looked-after children populations and, in the context of EI, it has been important to be clear about the benefits and limitations of the model. As such, the 'bottom line' has focused on supporting parents to meet the needs of their children and, in a neutral setting with professional support, families make important decisions and plan how they will support their child, and each other, in the future. This could be during a time of conflict, or where there is problematic behaviour or an important decision to be made about a child or young person's life. The focus is always firmly on the welfare of the child. The service has defined EI as occurring either at an early age or at an early stage of difficulties, and this has led to conferences being held involving children and young people across the 0- to 18-year spectrum and in relation to a broad range of issues.

One notable area of practice has focused on parental separation and divorce, and conferences related to these issues have produced the most promising outcomes. One key aspect of the success of FGC in this area may be linked to the clarity of purpose in the conference (the 'bottom line'). When parents separate or divorce we know that children are often caught in the complex adult issues and emotions with damaging results (Halpenny *et al.*, 2008). Issues such as contact, parenting styles and cooperative parenting to meet the children's needs can be difficult for parents to agree, particularly in acrimonious situations. The independence of the conference process, focusing on the needs of the children as opposed to the adult issues, is an important cornerstone. Often resolved through a legal process that begins with one party sending the other a solicitor's letter, FGC provides an alternative that allows parents control and the children's voices to be heard.

A second area of practice that the service has become involved in relates to supporting the parents of children with a disability, particularly at the EI stage of diagnosis. This can be a particularly stressful and confusing period in a family's life where the child's longer-term needs are difficult to clarify (Graungaard and Skov, 2007). With this group of service users, the service has found FGC particularly useful in mobilising the wider family network, and evaluations from families have pointed to reductions in stress. While longer-term evaluation would be required, managing the implications of stress on carers' mental health could only have positive benefits (McDermid and Holmes, 2013). Conferences have also been successfully held where disputes in relation to challenging adolescent behaviour have threatened family breakdown. These conferences have worked closely with

AfCs floating support service to maintain family relationships and prevent homelessness. This service is separately commissioned by the Supporting People Programme to prevent young people becoming homeless (www.nihe.gov.uk/index/corporate/supporting_people_ programme.htm/; accessed 20 February 2015). While much of the activity of the service is focused on supporting young people in their own tenancy, preventing young people being in this position is a key service aim and FGC has proved an invaluable tool in mediating family difficulties and involving the wider family circle.

Addressing the many difficulties faced by families in the FGC process has not been without challenges. Parental mental health difficulties and substance misuse are among the most prevalent and extend beyond the actual conference process. Enabling parents to focus on the needs of their children, agree a plan and then continue to stick with it can be problematic. The geographic area covered by the service also presents a major challenge of rural isolation, which can impact on parents in a number of ways; isolation can have a large impact on mental health and also makes access to services more difficult. The area is poorly served by public transport, so getting to and from services can be more challenging and AfC has addressed this through the provision of rural outreach. Conferences have also taken place in the family home where this has been assessed as appropriate.

Gaining extended family support in rural communities, heavily impacted by a recession, austerity and migration of a younger population, impacts directly on the longer-term effectiveness of plans. Developing a creative and responsive approach to family plans has been important, particularly in supporting families to come up with realistic rather than idealistic plans. Having the service closely linked with an Early Intervention Family Support Service and the development of Family Support Hubs has allowed for the wider picture of family needs to be considered as part of the next steps from the conference. The Health and Social Care Board has commissioned the development of Early Intervention Family Support Hubs, which are multi-agency and community based, to support the coordination of access to family support services at level two of the Northern Ireland Family Support Model.

AfC is responsible for coordinating the hubs in the same service area as the EI and FGC services. Provision of timely access to appropriate services, for children and adult family members, is a significant additional strength. The linkage between FGC and Family Support Hubs has also provided for a two-way referral process – FGC providing both an output referral route where family's needs are being considered within the Hub and an input referral for access to additional services. This concept of a family knowing and providing a solution, or at least an understanding of any additional needs, allows for a sense of empowerment for the family who are able to shape their own decision-making process.

The provision of FGC at an EI level has shown considerable promise and, in particular, the area of supporting families to plan for their children's needs in relation to key areas, such as separation, disability and risk of family breakdown, have produced positive outcomes. While longer-term research into the sustainability of plans is needed, re-referral rates to the service remain low and initial measurement of outcomes suggests that these have been positive in more than 80% of cases that went to conference.

The independence of the coordinator is a well-established principle in the case of many teams; as with the EI team, the role is often part of a single employer's remit. Promoting the coordinator's independent role within the team has been of key importance. This has allowed an independent approach to working with families, who may or may not be receiving additional support from the service. Working as part of an integrated team, providing EI support services to families and in conjunction with the Family Support Hubs, has enabled the broader remit of family needs to be addressed. The ability to work as part of this wider team has also reduced the risk of the coordinator becoming isolated. Working closely within the framework of wider AfC services provides a network of professional advice in areas such as safeguarding and the ability to signpost families. The quality of the coordinator's professional relationship, given the entirely voluntary nature of engagement, has also been a key cornerstone in the service. Unlike working within the remit of child protection registration, the motivation to address difficulties must rest almost entirely within the family's framework and motivation to change.

Southern HSCT: FrontLINE Assessment Service

One of the anticipated outcomes of the strategic policy direction outlined by the DHSSPS in *Care Matters* (DHSSPS, 2007) and *Families Matter* (DHSSPS, 2009a) was that, ultimately, there would be a reduction in the number of children admitted to state care. The desire to limit admissions to residential care, and to ensure an early return home if an admission does take place, is based on international, national and local research which confirms that children in residential care are among the most vulnerable in society to poorer outcomes (McMahon and Keenan, 2008). This was reflected in one of the targets set for HSCTs in 2009–2010 which required a reduction in emergency placements into residential care and stated that '90% of all children admitted to residential care should, prior to their admission ... have been the subject of a formal assessment to determine the need for residential care' (DHSSPS, 2009b, p. 15). This strategic direction has been reinforced by a more recent review of health and social care services in NI called *Transforming Your Care* (HSCB, 2011b). Among wide-ranging changes to all aspects of health and social care, this review prioritised services that focused on prevention, EI, greater choice and support for individual health and social care. In particular, it placed a requirement on HSCTs to reduce the need for residential childcare, by recommending that a review should be undertaken 'to minimise its necessity' (ibid., p. 88).

In line with this strategic objective, the Southern HSCT developed and piloted a new service which it named the Front Line Assessment Service. This recognised that EI not only focuses on the provision of early years services but can also take place at different key stages of social services intervention in the lives of children, young people and their families. Development of the service involved the identification of three dedicated foster care placements to be used for young people aged 12–17 years who would have previously been considered for admission to a residential assessment unit. A social worker with previous experience of the assessments used in residential care was appointed to work solely with the young people admitted to the new service. Being mindful of the vulnerability of young people in care, and specifically residential care, the aim of the service was to intervene as early and as decisively as possible on admission of a young person into care. The service works alongside the social worker with statutory responsibility, parents/carers and the family network to provide an intensive, robust and comprehensive assessment specifically address-ing the future placement needs of the young person within a six-week time frame. This highly resourced and focused assessment replaced the previous three-month time frame in residential care. The ser-vice achieves its aim by providing intensive, planned and supported strategies for rehabilitation in partnership with the young person, their family and community supports. Where a return home is not possible, it identifies the specific elements of placement required to meet the needs of the young person, thereby ensuring the best pos-sible match and therefore increasing the likelihood of a successful placement. This matching process is significant as stability for young people has been cited as a key factor to improve outcomes for children in care as placement breakdown results in multiple moves for young people (Teggart and Menary, 2005; VOYPIC, 2007).

From the commencement of the pilot in April 2011 to January 2014 there were forty-seven young people admitted, who had assess-ments completed in the Front Line Assessment Service. The outcomes for these young people were as follows:

- placed in foster care – 56% (n = 26);
- returned home – 36% (n = 17);
- placed in kinship care – 4% (n = 2);
- admitted to residential care – 2% (n = 1);
- independent living – 2% (n = 1).

The introduction of this service has contributed to a dramatic reduction in the number of young people being admitted to residen-tial care and, in particular, to the assessment/emergency facility. To put this into perspective, the proportion of looked-after children living in residential care in NI reduced from 13% in 2008 to 8% in 2013 (DHSSPS, 2013), but, within the Southern HSCT, this proportion is significantly less and has continued to fall – 7.1% in March 2011, 5.9% in March 2012, 4.3% in January 2014. While further research on the outcomes of the new service is required, the initial figures suggest a realistic, community-based alternative to residential care. In June 2013, as a direct result of this reduction in admissions to residential care (particularly emergency admissions), the trust closed its only emergency/assessment residential facility on a temporary basis to test the Front Line Assessment Service further. It has also contributed to a reduction in the maximum occupancy level in each of the remaining five longer-term residential units from seven to eight (depending on the unit) to five in each. The Southern HSCT is now the only trust in NI to have removed the need for a residential unit for emergency admissions with admissions to residential care occurring only on a planned basis.

Although not an integrated component of the service, FGC has been introduced in a small number of cases during the pilot period. Its use in these cases has been noted to bring added value to the process of planning supported strategies for rehabilitation home or identifying the most appropriate alternative placement to meet the needs of the young person concerned. This added value arises from the success of FGC in involving the wider family network in planning and decision-making and in harnessing their knowledge and support. A number of research studies have found that the use of FGC leads to a reduction in the need for children to be placed in state care, as family placements are more frequently offered (Wilmot, 2000; Gunderson et al., 2003; Titcomb and LeCroy, 2005). This was also evidenced in NI with one HSCT reporting fifteen children returned home from care and thirty-seven family placements offered, thereby diverting children from care (FGCFNI, 2012). These findings would suggest the benefits of intensive EI, involving family members in decision-making, should not be underestimated. Velen and Devine (2005) found that, in comparison to more traditional interventions, there was more than double the number of family members available to offer assistance to a young person when FGC is used. Of significant note is that young people who were in the care system for protracted periods of time reported feeling amazed and grateful at the number of family members who took an interest and attended meetings about their care and well-being.

The Front Line Assessment Service within the Southern HSCT has, to date, demonstrated early evidence of a viable alternative to admitting young people aged 12–17 years to residential care. In the context of plans to expand the service to younger children, it has been helpful to reflect on the benefits brought by the use of FGC and how its use could be extended and introduced in a more integrated way to achieve positive outcomes.

Conclusion

The examples outlined above indicate that, in the context of EI, FGC is a promising practice. The model is flexible and can be used either as an integral component of an EI initiative, as in the AfC Early Intervention Service, or as a complementary approach, as in the Front Line Assessment Service in the Southern HSCT. It can also be introduced in response to a wide range of difficulties and presenting issues at different levels of need (Mulhern, 1996; Pennell and Burford, 2000; Wilmot, 2000; Merkel-Holguin *et al.*, 2007). Research also suggests that FGC is viewed positively by families in comparison to other, more traditional methods (Marsh and Crow, 1998; Holland *et al.*, 2005).

The most advantageous aspect of the model, however, is its ability to involve parents, children and young people – and wider family and community networks – in developing plans to address their own issues and difficulties. Graybeal (2001) argues that if families can be supported to identify their own strengths and those available to them within the community then the outcomes will improve over the longer term (see also Dolan *et al.*, 2015, Chapter 4 in this volume). This empowering aspect of the model is in harmony with the intentions of the *Families Matter* strategy in NI which states:

> DHSSPS wants to involve children, young people, their families and communities in the development of preventive services. We want children, young people and their families to be empowered with the skills and knowledge to protect themselves ... develop the confidence and capability to love, protect and care for their community and family members (DHSSPS, 2009a, p. 16).

However, a final cautionary note: while early evidence would support the position that the FGC model has a strong focus on engaging family members, its longer term impact on lasting change and outcomes is harder to quantify (Huntsman, 2006; Barnsdale and Walker, 2007; Crampton, 2007). Perhaps in part the difficulty lies in the short-term nature of the intervention. Unlike other types of family support intervention, the coordinator's role with the family is seldom continued beyond the conference, except for a planned review. As such, the long-term viability of the plan is reliant on the family's ability to stick with it, and this can be weakened if appropriate mechanisms are not put in place to monitor and review the plan developed by the family group (Hoy, unpublished). As outlined in Figure 5.1 above, these arrangements need to be seen as integral to the FGC process with clear agreement reached about how the plan will be monitored and reviewed in order to increase its potential for success. With that said, the flexibility and strengths of the FGC model indicate that the potential for its wider use within EI initiatives should be explored further.

CHAPTER 6

Empowering vulnerable and troubled families: Area Family Support Teams in Walsall

Sharon Vincent

Introduction

This chapter discusses a new approach to delivering children's services through Area Family Support Teams (AFSTs) in Walsall and outlines some of the outcomes that have been achieved for vulnerable families who received support from these teams. The author undertook an independent analysis of the impact of the support provided by the first AFST to be established (Vincent, 2013) and the discussion in this chapter focuses on the findings from this analysis. The research included qualitative longitudinal tracking of fifteen case study families and identification of key stakeholder perspectives. It was also informed by an internal economic evaluation undertaken by the council's finance department.

The local authority

Walsall is one of seven metropolitan boroughs within the West Midlands conurbation, a heavily urbanised region in western central England. The borough suffers from high unemployment and high levels of child poverty and has some of the most economically deprived communities in the UK. Its infant mortality rates are among the highest in the country. There was a pressing local need to drive down costs within this local authority. The average length of stay in care had increased from two and a half to four years in the four years prior to 2009/10, and the projected financial benefits of investing a comparably small amount of money in family intervention services were compelling.

A new approach to providing children's services

A new operating model for children's services was introduced. It was aimed at reducing cost by refocusing resources into prevention, providing a robust offer of early help to vulnerable families and coordinating the resources and services delivering secondary prevention to free capacity to empower local people working on local solutions to meet local need. The new approach was influenced by evidence of what works and supports key elements of the government's national policy approach to vulnerable and troubled families including EI and a whole family approach, multi-agency working, promoting the role of families, peers and community champions, and expansion of the role of non-state service providers (HM Government 2010; Ministry of Justice, 2010; Allen and Duncan Smith, 2010; HM Government, 2011a; HM Government, 2011b; Munro, 2011). It:

- addresses the context of vulnerability and takes account of the wider processes of disadvantage impacting on vulnerable and troubled families and communities in which they are located including lack of employment and training opportunities, poor physical environments, inappropriate housing conditions, limited household income, financial problems and debt, and domestic violence;
- ensures that intensive family intervention is based on a holistic, whole family approach with coordination between statutory services, voluntary services and the local community and families themselves;
- recognises the need for local areas to have freedom and flexibility to pool funding in order to provide personalised packages of support for vulnerable and troubled families.

Figure 6.1. is an illustration of the support pathway that was used by the local authority at the time the research was undertaken (it now uses levels 1-4 in line with other local authorities). It identifies different levels of need – from those that can be met by universal services through to those that require statutory intervention:

- Level 0 – The Child Concern and the Healthy Child Model define this group as well children accessing universal services such as health, education and leisure provision and who make good overall progress in all areas of development;

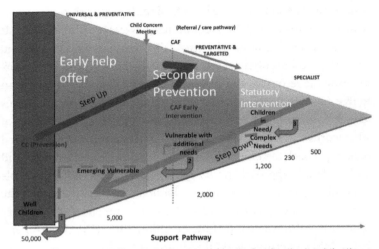

Figure 6.1 The support pathway which was used by the local authority at the time the research was undertaken by the author.

- Level 1 – Children and young people who require some extra support in the form of an 'Early Help Offer' from a single-agency targeted service because they live in households where parenting capacity is not fully meeting their needs which may impact on their overall health and development;
- Level 2 – Children whose health and development is at risk of being impaired who require a secondary, preventive, multi-agency, integrated response to meet these needs using Child Concern and CAF procedures;
- Level 3 – Children who are at high risk of impairment or who have experienced significant harm or are at risk of significant harm and require a multi-agency response from statutory services with social care taking the lead.

The plan was to reduce the number of children whose needs become more complex and have to be 'stepped up' to statutory services (level three) as well as to increase the number of children whose needs could be met with an offer of early help by being 'stepped down' (to level two).

Changing systems and cultures

The new operating model was based on the joining up of all aspects of children's services and partner agencies and the reshaping of services across traditional boundaries. The model is a TAF approach involving engagement with the whole family in which families' views are central to decision-making. The non-judgemental approach is one of the programme's main strengths since families are more likely to engage if they feel they are being listened to and are able to influence the support package. The Department for Communities and Local Government (DCLG) argues that staff engaged in family intervention must:

> ... look at the family from the inside out, to understand its dynamics as a whole, and to offer practical help and support – but also to be the person to authoritatively challenge that family to change (DCLG, 2013).

AFST practitioners have worked in this way. They have been assertive as well as non-judgemental, taking a fair but firm approach to tackling difficult issues with families.

The new way of working is an integrated approach to prevention that addresses risk and protective factors and targets all ecological levels – the individual, the family and the community. It is a solution-focused, resilience-based approach that seeks to empower families by equipping them with critical coping skills. By enhancing family and community strengths the expectation was that family functioning should be sustainable over time.

Multi-agency AFSTs located within children's centres, local schools or other buildings accessible to the local community were established across the local authority. The teams were designed to include a centre manager, children's social worker, family support workers, targeted youth support worker, health visitor, adult community worker and CAF coordinator, but the actual composition of the teams changed over time in response to identified client need: for example, a welfare rights adviser was brought in to provide support when it became apparent that almost all families had benefit and debt issues. Although the AFSTs were multi-agency, dedicated health visitor input was not achieved in every team and the teams acknowledged that dedicated mental health service support would have been useful.

It might have been expected that integrating staff from different professions would have proved challenging, yet frontline staff have fully embraced the new way of working and professional boundaries and traditional silos have been broken down and links between adult and child's services have been strengthened, creating a more seamless service within which adult and child workers cooperate in helping the whole family. Time has been built in for peer support and practice reflection, and staff really value this and report that they feel more confident in challenging other members of the team, as well as external colleagues. This is really important since professional challenge is one of the key requisites of a successful child protection system.

Locating the AFSTs in locally accessible places, such as schools, has meant that other agencies can drop in and speak to them and this has also been hugely beneficial. The teams believe this has resulted in their innovative way of working filtering through to external agencies, with other agencies now recognising that, in order to improve things for children, there is a need to obtain the views of and engage everyone in the family. They have also been able to offer important safeguarding advice to staff in universal services, thereby preventing a number of inappropriate child protection referrals.

AFSTs offer a range of universal, targeted and specialist services to children and families proportionate to their needs. Direct support includes emotional, practical and financial support. AFSTs provide key items including food, money for heating and essential furniture items. Such emergency support has been essential in cases where the social security system has failed to adequately safeguard children from poverty. A number of families who come to the attention of the AFSTs have no money for food or heating because they have no income, apart from child benefit, because their benefits have been suspended. Other families, particularly large families, have more stable incomes from social security benefits but lack essential items such as beds and cots. In addition to providing emergency financial support, the AFSTs can provide financial help in situations where existing support systems are unable to meet families' needs. For example, they have funded counselling sessions for young people and secured funding from children's services for alternative education resources for young people not engaging in school, when education authorities have refused or been unable to provide support.

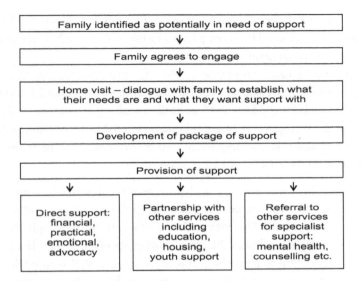

Figure 6.2 The support process

The AFSTs also provide practical support to families: for example, by transporting children to school or attending children's medical appointments with parents. This form of support is crucial in terms of promoting continuity of education, promoting children's health and well-being and preventing medical neglect. The teams also accompany parents to GP appointments, mental health appointments and specialist drug and alcohol service appointments, which is also important since children are likely to be better protected and cared for if their parents' mental health is stable and they are engaging effectively with mental health and substance misuse services (Vincent, 2012).

Children's social workers have played a crucial role in the AFSTs in terms of ensuring safeguarding. Family support workers have skills in promoting effective family functioning and have been particularly effective in tackling parenting issues and inadequate home conditions. The AFSTs have promoted independence by taking parents shopping and helping them cook; identified safety risks in the home; provided bins, skips and storage to facilitate improvements in home conditions; provided childcare; promoted engagement in social activities to prevent parents' social isolation;

and provided peer engagement opportunities for children. They have also mediated between parents to promote more harmonious contact arrangements for children.

An initial focus on practical help – for example, getting repairs done, providing a skip to clear rubbish or obtaining essential items, such as beds for children or a functioning washing machine or cooker – has been important in enabling a relationship to be built with families, and this is an important step in bringing about permanent change. As the DCLG (2012, p. 21) points out:

> Seeing some practical and quick results can signal to families that the worker intends to keep their promises and is there to help. This may be the point where families begin to see their worker as different to other agencies in their lives and begin to trust them and become more willing to work with them … Small improvements such as a cleaner house or garden are often a critical first step forward for families. These improvements can reduce other problems such as depression or difficult family relationships that can be exacerbated by poor living conditions as well as improving a family's motivation to make bigger changes.

Although they work with the whole family, the AFSTs assess the individual needs of each family member and provide one-to-one support for individual family members. For example, they have given emotional support for individual children or advice around the impact of risky behaviour for teenagers, and youth workers have played a key role in this type of support.

The AFSTs have also had an important advocacy role. They have liaised with housing agencies to prevent eviction; have ensured urgent repairs are carried out, particularly those that constitute safety risks to children and vulnerable adults; and have assisted families to move to more appropriate accommodation. They have also acted as advocates to seek financial, benefit, debt and employment advice for vulnerable parents. This kind of support cannot be overestimated since poverty can be a significant stress factor for parents, which, when combined with other stressors, can impede parents' capacity to protect their children (Brandon *et al.*, 2002;

Vincent, 2010). AFSTs have also advocated for young people and their parents when there have been education issues. This has included listening to young people's views when schools have failed to do so; ensuring parents are able to express their views; and sourcing alternative education places for young people to promote reengagement with education. This does, however, beg the question of whether the AFSTs have had to assume responsibilities that should have been the responsibility of education. AFSTs have also acted as advocates for parents with literacy and numeracy issues whose problems were magnified because they were unable to read or understand letters that were sent to them from schools, housing or the Department for Work and Pensions (DWP) and have sourced literacy and numeracy classes for young people and parents to increase their future employment capabilities and promote readiness for work.

The AFSTs were never expected to meet all the needs of families within their own team. Partnership working is essential and the teams have built up good relationships with other services. They have been able to identify need more quickly and have referred adults and children to a number of specialist services including mental health, specialist youth services, counselling and smoking cessation ones.

The AFSTs were given the flexibility to think 'outside the box' in order to meet families' needs, and this has enabled them to respond to some unusual service requests: for example, they paid for a hotel room for a family for a night and secured a vicar to bless the house when a mother refused to return home because she believed her house was possessed by evil spirits; they arranged for the locks to be changed on a house to prevent a mother's ex-husband entering at will; and they arranged for child benefit to be paid to a father rather than a mother in order to prevent the mother spending the money on alcohol. Having their own dedicated budgets has been crucial in enabling the AFSTs to meet these kinds of needs and to prevent problems escalating.

Another positive has been that the AFSTs have not been constrained by thresholds and traditional referral routes, which inevitably operate to exclude a certain number of families who need help. This has meant they have been able to work with:

- families with high levels of need who might be expected to become at risk of referral to statutory services without intensive, multi-agency support to prevent escalation of their needs;
- families whose needs are not being met by existing service providers either because they fall below existing thresholds or because they have simply fallen through the net and have been unable to receive a service from any agency;
- families who are receiving support but where existing service providers have either been unsuccessful in engaging them or have been unable to make any positive impact on their lives.

AFSTs have worked with a diverse range of families with multiple and complex issues, including large and small ones; families that include older adult children and grandparents; one-parent families headed up by males and females; traditional, two-parent families; step-parent families; families from different ethnic groups; and parents of different sexualities. They have cooperated with all family members including grandparents and adult children and have been particularly successful at engaging and sustaining engagement with large families with complex needs. This is important because evidence suggests that children in large families may be at greater risk of harm, particularly neglect (Brandon *et al.*, 2009; Vincent, 2012). In comparison with many other interventions, AFSTs have had a high level of success in engaging males including fathers, adult male children and teenage boys. This is partly because male workers have been appointed to some of the teams, but even all-female teams have had considerable success in engaging males.

A small number of families that the teams worked with had less entrenched needs and might have been expected to have received support through other channels: for example, families where the primary presenting issue was that parents were having difficulty transporting children to school due to ill health. Such families did not present with multiple underlying issues, were not troubled families, would not in usual circumstances have been considered vulnerable and were not hard to engage. It is unlikely that they would ever have been stepped up to child protection but they were temporarily vulnerable due to their own health issues or those of their children. In normal circumstances, they could cope perfectly well but exceptional ones had led them to require additional support and existing support systems were so inflexible that they could not offer the help the families needed. By working with them, the AFSTs exposed a number of systems issues that needed to be rectified. Hopefully, in the future, the kinds of support that these families needed will be met by universal services, thereby freeing up this highly skilled, multi-agency team to work with families with more complex issues.

Families' journeys

The lives of vulnerable troubled families are often characterised by periods of crisis, disengagement and regression, and pathways to change are not straightforward. As Flint *et al.* (2011) point out, the terminology of 'journey' for a vulnerable family does not necessarily imply a linear pathway of change or progress. Figure 6.3 outlines the characteristics of one of the families who were supported by an AFST, describes the kinds of support they received and summarises their 'journey'.

Case Study Family A

Family A had already been identified as a child concern case by the local authority when they were referred to the AFST by the children's centre. Although the children were well cared for and there were no concerns about mum's parenting skills, the parents had recently separated and there were concerns about domestic violence and financial abuse; dad had been physically abusive to the children as well as to mum; and his drinking was a concern. There were also housing issues, particularly problems with overcrowding. Mum worked sixteen hours a week but her older adult children were unemployed and her oldest son had threatened suicide. The ten-year-old child received speech and language support as well as help from a youth worker for behavioural issues at school.

When the AFST met the family, mum said she wanted help to get her older sons motivated to look for work and help with her daughter's non-attendance at school. She had previously been taken to court for her son's non-attendance. She was struggling to cope with her ten-year-old son's behavioural issues and her two younger children were also displaying aggressive behaviour and swearing and fighting. She wanted help with benefits and debts, a bed for one of her younger children and more space. One of the adult sons wanted help finding work as he had never worked before, and he also would have liked his own home; the other was seeking

The family (White British)
Mum; 3 adult sons 21, 20 and 18; girl 16; boy 10; boy 8; girl 6

Issues the family wanted support with:
- Employment
- Financial problems
- Education
- Parenting/household issues
- Housing

Other presenting or emerging issues:
- Domestic violence
- Sibling abuse

Support provided:

Direct support
- Financial support: paid for the locks to be changed, provided bed and brownie uniform, paid for alternative education place
- Practical support: provided transport for the daughter and older sons
- Family support: gave mum advice on routines and behaviour, helped her develop mealtime rotas; provided childcare

Advocacy
- Benefits advice, debt advice, employment advice
- Arranged for housing repairs to be undertaken
- Attended school meetings

Referral to other services
- Referral to targeted youth support
- Referral to CAMHS

Outcomes:
- Reduction in offending (mum prevented from going to court for child's non-attendance)
- Prevention of eviction
- Increased participation in employment (mum and eldest son)
- Stabilisation of mental health issues (child referred to appropriate services, no further instances of self-harm)
- Reductions in behavioural problems (child's conflict and anger issues reduced)
- Increased participation/attainment in education
- Improved parenting skills
- Poverty reduction – family claiming all benefits they are entitled to and debts managed
- Engagement in social activities (youngest child)
- Increased confidence (mum)

Figure 6.3 Family A

an apprenticeship. The sixteen year old wished to do voluntary work with a nursery or administrative work.

The AFST worked with this family for almost eight months before stepping them down to universal support: '… everyone's skills within our core team have been utilised'. Everyone 'stepped outside their comfort zones to work with this family'.

There were a number of crises during the period of support. Initially, the AFST felt support for mum would be the best way to impact on the ten year old's behavioural problems but when he threatened self-harm they secured a targeted support worker for him and arranged for his GP to make a referral to Child and Adolescent Mental Health Services (CAMHS). The AFST were able to make sure the referral happened much more quickly than would have been the case in the old, less joined-up way of working. The targeted support worker made a child protection referral after the young person told him he had threatened self-harm, but the AFST were able to explain their involvement with the family and prevent the case from escalating. There were also potential sibling abuse issues after the boy told the targeted youth worker that his twenty-one-year-old brother had hit him and burnt him with a cigarette. The AFST followed up these allegations but believed mum's account that he had burnt himself.

The AFST concluded that mum should get 'a medal for what she's achieved'. By the time they closed the case she was working full time and thinking about setting up her own business. She was more confident and assertive and put the needs of her younger children first. The sixteen year old engaged really well with the team. They established that she did not want to go back to school, attended school meetings with her and ensured her views were expressed, found alternative education for her and secured funding for this after the school refused to pay. The adult sons also engaged. The AFST facilitated employment advice for them and took them to appointments and one found and sustained employment. The team also sorted out mum's housing benefit and helped her with money management.

Mum described the help she received as 'brilliant'. Her lead worker was known to her because she had previously been her family support worker for three years so she was able to compare the quality of support she received from the AFST with that she had received before, which 'never really got anywhere … there was only so much family support could do … now you mention a problem and they're on to it, it's sorted … every problem they're on it'.

She felt the AFST were able to offer far more than traditional family support: for example, when she needed the locks changed on her doors because her husband had been coming in and out all day and she was unable to fund this, 'they got it done … family support couldn't have done that'. As a result she said she now felt safer. She believed that it was much better to deal with problems in a 'cluster' rather than respond to individual issues. She liked the fact that 'the kids are involved with decisions — it's giving them a choice, they've been given a choice in what they do'. If it had not been for the help she had received from the AFST she said she would have had to attend court because her daughter had not been attending school. 'They've supported [her daughter] a lot, it's what she needed, they got her motivated, she got no help before.' She also appreciated the time she got to spend with her ten-year-old son when the team arranged childcare for the other children because she said it was hard to spend time alone with an individual child in such a large family. The AFST had also sorted out her rent arrears when she had been threatened with eviction and given her the confidence to stick to routines with her children.

The sixteen year old was really appreciative of the support she received:

> I was having problems at school, I'd been out of school for ages ...
> No one at school was helping ... I felt really uncomfortable when
> I had to go to meetings at school ... They wouldn't let me explain
> how I felt. They wouldn't let me put what I thought on the table.

She said when the AFST came to speak to her it was the first time she had been able to articulate what she wanted in terms of education. She said she loved the alternative education placement the team secured for her:

> I can get one-on-one help there which is what I need; at school there
> was no help at all ... They tell me I'm capable of getting qualifica-
> tions here so I make the effort to do the work.

She said she would not have sat two GCSEs without the support from the AFST. She also felt the AFST had helped her mum and her older siblings:

> My brothers are going to interviews now which is a big improve-
> ment. They would never have bothered looking for stuff otherwise.
> They're looking at apprenticeships. They would never have done
> that before.

Outcomes and sustainability

The AFSTs work with families for an average of 4.7 months, but in some cases for as long as ten months. This is a significant length of time for what is intended to be short-term intensive intervention, but for some families – particularly large families with very complex issues – this is appropriate. Some families faced issues such as severe deterioration in mental health and even made suicide attempts during the time the AFSTs worked with them, and it would not have been appropriate to withdraw support for these families any earlier.

Crisis management is crucial in terms of preventing situations escalating and is essential in achieving transformative change. One of the key roles of the AFSTs has been around crisis management.

Although 'achieving change' is the main focus of an intervention and 'hard' transformative outcomes are, therefore, important, improving the stability of families and reducing immediate risk of harm and responding to trauma are significant outcomes in their own right. The AFSTs have demonstrated that they are well placed to do this and are able to reduce immediate risks of harm, thereby stabilising risky situations. Because they see families in their home regularly, often on a daily basis at the start of the intervention, the AFSTs are arguably in a better position than any other service to monitor families and respond to early warning signs. Because they work with the whole family, they can monitor mental and emotional health and risk of suicide, the domestic environment, family relationships and dynamics, conflict with peers and neighbours, and school attendance. They can even keep an eye on levels of alcohol and drug use and are, therefore, very well placed to work with substance-misusing families that are being stepped down from statutory support.

AFSTs can ensure parents take children to medical appointments and can identify and respond to escalating child protection situations in families with young children. Unlike many other interventions, they can also identify and respond to risky sexual or other behaviour among adolescents.

Lastly, AFSTs have the ability to identify and respond to systems-related risks, such as withdrawal of services, or benefit sanctions. This monitoring role is key in local authorities such as this one where health visitors who would traditionally provide surveillance of pre-school children are in such short supply and where some school-age children appear to have become lost in the education service because of the move to academies. The AFSTs identified a number of children who were not attending school and ensured they became reengaged with education. The sixteen-year-old girl who was discussed in the case example in Figure 6.3 had not attended school for two years, and if her family had not come to the attention of the AFST she would probably have remained out of education. As a result of the support the AFST provided, she went on to sit GCSEs and planned to attend college. Thus, there may be huge long-term savings over her lifetime.

Very few cases the AFST work with are closed due to non-engagement. A small number are appropriately stepped up to child protection, and, while this might be seen as a negative outcome, these escalations to child protection are likely to be made at an earlier stage than would have been the case without the AFSTs so families are receiving appropriate support at an earlier stage. Most cases that are closed are stepped down to support from universal services but a small number remain open to child concern.

The range of issues that are required to be addressed by the AFSTs indicates the scale of the challenges facing the families they work with and illustrates the difficulties they face in actually achieving transformative change. Although the intervention is 'intensive' and may involve providing greater levels of resources to families than traditional services, there is a need to be realistic about what the AFSTs can actually achieve. There is, however, evidence that some of the families that the teams have worked with have travelled huge distances in a relatively short time. The AFSTs have undeniably turned around the lives of vulnerable and troubled families with multiple problems, and families are unanimous in stating that their involvement with the AFST has been positive and linked to achievement of sustainable outcomes.

Hard, transformative outcomes which have been gained include:
- improvements in educational attendance and attainment;
- entry to training, education or employment;
- reduction or cessation of risky behaviour;
- reduction or cessation of criminal behaviour;
- prevention of eviction.

Some young people continued, however, not to attend school, and some parents were facing court for non-attendance at the time the case was closed or after the case closed, while other families made limited progress in addressing underlying issues, such as parenting or substance misuse.

Few families displayed linear progression towards sustainable outcomes. Rather, it was more often the case that there were periods of progress followed by episodes of crisis or setback, and then subsequent progress again. Many of the positive outcomes identified were 'soft', and related to crisis management and stabilisation of families rather than achieving transformative change.

'Soft' outcomes which were accomplished include:

- improved self-confidence/self-esteem;
- improved mental health;
- improved domestic environments;
- improved inter-familial relationships and dynamics;
- improved personal and social skills;
- raised aspirations.

Conclusion

Although there were demonstrable hard and soft outcomes there are challenges in charting 'progress', attributing causality and identifying quantifiable or measurable outcomes. It is hard to say what the outcomes for these families would have been anyway and what can actually be attributed to the AFSTs because it is difficult to isolate the work of the AFST, especially as the child concern and CAF process often continued in parallel with AFST involvement.

It is also challenging to predict whether outcomes can be sustained over time. Many families were affected by mental health issues, which can be unpredictable in nature and result in periods of crisis. Some of the families that the AFSTs worked with had young children and, while the teams were able to address the issues these families had at this stage in their lives, it is possible some of the children might face different problems, which will impact on family functioning once they are at school. National benefit changes will also have significant impacts on some of these families and they may encounter difficulties if, for example, they come off benefits and participate in employment, but for one reason or another are unable to sustain this.

Lastly, there were a number of lone-parent families whose lives were stable at the time that the AFSTs stopped working with them but risks to mothers and children can change dramatically at any time if, for example, a violent male moves into a household (Vincent, 2010). Some of the families that the AFSTs have worked with will inevitably need additional support in times of crisis, and there is a need to ensure that this is well understood and that the intervention is not deemed a failure if families are referred for additional support in the future.

CHAPTER 7

Love Barrow Families: A case study of transforming public services

Katrina Robson, Alison Tooby and Robbie Duschinsky

Introduction

This chapter describes the development of Love Barrow Families, a new way of working with complex families in the community of Barrow-in-Furness, Cumbria in England. The project recognises the significance of relationships and connection at an early stage, i.e. before problems reach the threshold of services. This means that 'intervening' can be thought about in a way that captures the assets which already exist in neighbourhood and community. Love Barrow Families is rooted in the community and has grown from the ground upwards. This chapter describes the role of co-production in providing a framework and source of inspiration during the two years that the project has been running. It also shows how the project has been informed by the Dynamic Maturational Model (DMM) of Attachment, a theory of human development and set of assessments which have helped us understand and respond to the complexities of families' lives. The principles of co-production and the DMM have worked well together because both recognise the fundamental nature of relationships for the mental and physical well-being of families, neighbourhoods and communities.

Transforming Public Services
The problem

In a small community such as Barrow-in-Furness, families who face the most complex problems are comparatively easily identified. Although only a small percentage of the population, local practitioners point out that they receive a large number of services but often have the poorest outcomes. This picture has been reflected nationally (C4EO, 2011; DCFS, 2009): projects such as the English government's Troubled Families initiative have consistently highlighted the cost to society and the need to find more effective ways of working with families with complex requirements. Since the 2000s, it had become increasingly clear that, although the number of services involved with these families had vastly increased, the same families appeared time and time again at the door of our agencies. This often left the professionals feeling frustrated and perplexed. In the same period, frontline workers felt the pressure of the increasing focus on targets and paperwork, leaving even less time to get to know and understand families or communicate effectively with other agencies involved (Munro, 2011).

For this small percentage of families with the most complex problems, the need to understand their situation properly before beginning any intervention plan is crucial, both in terms of better outcomes for the family and to ensure a more efficient, orderly and economical use of resources. Effective understanding of the issues facing a whole family is reduced, and even sometimes seriously undermined, because assessments are undertaken by separate adult and child services, focusing on either the needs of the parent or those of the child, rather than on both. Mental health and social care requirements are also artificially split, reflecting the focus of different organisations. Interventions are also usually determined by the services available in a team rather than what is needed from a family perspective.

For many families, the interventions received in the past had not addressed their problems and any apparent progress had not been sustained. Too often this had resulted in years of futile (and expensive) work that ended with children coming into the care system, where they often did not fulfil their potential and were over-represented in mental health and treatment services (DES, 2006).

Barrow-in-Furness is an industrial town with a population of approximately 70,000 and is located on the south-west tip of the county of Cumbria. The county is in the north-west of England and is predominantly rural, containing the Lake District and Lake District National Park, which is considered one of England's most outstanding areas of natural beauty.

Barrow-in-Furness is currently among the 10% most economically deprived districts in England. The town has a history of steelwork and shipbuilding, and the main employer is BAE Systems. The effects of the recent major economic and political changes in the UK have led to a widening gap in terms of the distribution of wealth, poverty, inequality and social mobility (Ferragina *et al.*, 2013). One result has been the further exclusion and isolation of a small number of families within their communities. Furthermore, in these times of austerity, cutbacks have meant that services across the country have had to focus increasingly on tightening referral criteria and drawing lines between their service and other services – with the outcome of further fragmentation of service delivery and a 'refer on' mentality. Some of these difficulties have been highlighted as failings in a number of Serious Case Reviews which have resulted, locally and nationally, in professionals being urged to 'share information and agree action' (Cumbria Local Safeguarding Children Board, 2012; see also Vincent, 2010).

The ideas

The scheme for the Love Barrow Families has not developed overnight. Setting up a project such as this has taken a lifetime of experience and learning within the community of families and professionals in Barrow-in-Furness, and close attention to the wider national and global context. Starting from what it means to be Barrovian and reflecting the unique strengths and issues faced by our community have been paramount. The French philosopher Simone Weil wrote that: 'to be rooted is perhaps the most important and least recognised need of the human soul' (Weil, 1955, p. 40). This sense of belonging and knowing where we come from is something that has been passed on through generations of families in Barrow and remains true to this day. The loyalty, goodness and pride most people here feel in belonging to the borough of Barrow-in-Furness has been a strong foundation from which to build. Strengthening resilience through connection with family, neighbourhood and community so that families who need extra help are supported before they come to the door of mental health or social services seems a more productive use of resources for everyone.

It has also been important to us to bring together and use theories, research and evidence to inform what we do in a way that connects to real life and makes sense to ordinary people. Dr John Howarth has been an inspiration and a source of knowledge and experience, encouraging us to bring to life ideas from asset-based working (Kretzmann and McKnight, 1993), thinking about the assets in our own community. Dr Julia Slay from the New Economics Foundation helped us to understand and implement co-production principles (Boyle and Harris, 2009).

Another major source of inspiration for Love Barrow Families has been the DMM of Attachment and Adaptation (Crittenden, 2008). The DMM was introduced to the Barrow community at a well-attended, five-day Attachment and Psychopathology course in 2005 and has since found a home there, becoming embedded in the practice and minds of many professionals across different agencies. A few of us have trained extensively with Dr Patricia Crittenden in using her assessments, such as the Adult Attachment Interview (AAI), the CARE-Index and the School Age Assessment of Attachment (SAA) to understand relationships in complex families so that intervention can identify and address underlying problems (Robson & Savage, 2001; Robson & Tooby, 2004; Robson & Wetherell, 2011). This includes intervening in practical and therapeutic ways and also targeting the intervention towards the child and/or the adults as needed. Furthermore, a research study carried out in Barrow with the support of Cumbria Partnership Foundation Trust meant fifty families in Barrow assisted the development of the DMM ideas by volunteering to participate in the longitudinal research (Crittenden *et al.*, 2015, forthcoming). Half of these families were complex and known to agencies. This research showed that attachment issues in children and, especially parents, underlay a large majority of children's behavioural problems; identifying these attachment issues offered a new and more effective way to understand the family problems and guided professionals in their interventions. In addition, they discovered that the most troubled families were also the those who wanted to give the most to the research – in the hope that professionals could use their experience to help others.

Implementing ideas: The Love Barrow families project

Support for the initial idea came from the Cumbria Partnership NHS Foundation Trust, which employed Katrina Robson. The Cumbria

Partnership NHS Foundation Trust is the largest provider of NHS services in the county of Cumbria. It employs around four thousand staff, who operate sixty community and mental health services from around twenty main sites and other premises that are shared with other health and community services such as GP surgeries. It is one of 147 foundation trusts in England. NHS foundation trusts are not-for-profit, public-benefit corporations. They are part of the NHS and provide more than half of all NHS hospital, mental health and ambulance services.

Foundation trusts are not directed by government so have greater freedom to decide, with their governors and members, their own strategy and the way services are run. They can retain their surpluses and borrow to invest in services for patients and service users. They are accountable to their local communities through their members and governors and commissioners through contracts and Parliament. They are inspected by the Independent Care Quality Commission and overseen by Monitor, an independent regulator.

The Love Barrow Families project team also sought support from key stakeholders in Cumbria County Council, which is the local authority for the county of Cumbria and was established in 1974, following its first elections held a year before. It is an elected local government body responsible for the most significant local services in the county, including children's services.

A talk from Dr John Howarth, Executive Director for Integration, Cumbria Partnership Foundation Trust, in 2011 led to further discussion and a plan for a short, time-limited piece of work with frontline professionals and families. The plan won second place in an innovation competition held by the trust, which granted funding for the preliminary piece of work. Co-production principles were followed in the design of the project and remain at its heart. This reflected the need for a new approach that recognised that people's requirements are better met when they are involved in a reciprocal relationship with professionals and others, working together to get things done.

In these early stages, a group of complex families from Barrow-in-Furness was identified and asked if they would be willing to come together with Katrina Robson and Alison Tooby to share experiences and document the things that they had found the most helpful from services and the things that had been unhelpful. The work of John Seddon (2008) and Mark Friedman (2009) informed this process. The group included a spread of families, some of whom had had involvement with agencies for generations and had experienced significant health and social care problems, and some of whom were foster parents and had supported troubled children and their families. During a series of three meetings, this group used quality and service improvement tools, such as root cause analysis (NHS Institute for Innovation and Improvement, 2007), to reach a consensus about how agencies could best help families and documented their five top priorities.

At the same time, a group of local, multi-agency, frontline professionals also had three meetings, going through a similar process of looking at what they felt was working currently and what needed to be changed in order to better meet the needs of complex families. This group included community and third-sector organisations and both adult and child services across health and social care. One of the interesting things that happened was a recognition from a number of professionals that some of our own families were also complex. From this, a small number of colleagues were able to influence the project by sharing their own experience of being on the receiving end of services. This demonstrated the power of the co-production principles and allowed professionals to acknowledge and think about themselves and the impact of their own history on their work.

Families' top five priorities

· What do we need from services?
- compassion and understanding;
- a team that joins up services for children with services for parents and that provides twenty-four-hour support if and when needed;
- services developed in our local community which are available for when families ask for help e.g. using older experienced members of the community to 'foster' and support the whole family unit rather than children being taken into foster care;
- to *not* have to live in fear of having our children taken away. We need honesty and clarity about what needs to change in

order to keep our children safe and the right help to make these changes;

- an honest and equal trusting relationship with one main professional.

Frontline professionals' top five areas
How can we best meet the needs of families?

- a local initiative that joins up services for whole families, bringing together adult and child services;
- one clear assessment tool for a whole family;
- to have less paperwork and more time to spend with families so that we can respond when it is needed and for as long as needed;
- to feel safe within a team that can work with families to hold and address risk as part of our day-to-day work, i.e. services can be provided to families whether or not they need to be subject to safeguarding procedures;
- to have high-quality supervision, training and guidance provided by experienced professionals who can act as mentors and who can support ongoing care planning and evaluation.

The fourth meeting brought both groups together, with the families presenting their ideas to the professionals who also shared their thoughts. The meeting was also attended by one of the non-executive directors of Cumbria Partnership Foundation Trust, reflecting the need to ensure communication from the bottom to the top of the organisation. The families were treated as experts in their problems and in how services had affected them. The professionals were considered experts in the work of their particular agency and in how to identify and address problems. Both families and professionals appeared to feel good about this work. It was an auspicious basis on which to build a new way of working together. Lessons learnt from integrating services in Torbay (Thistlethwaite, 2011) underlined the significance of having a clear vision based on views of service users, bringing together frontline staff and the local community and having the support of early joint governance and senior management.

The next step was, therefore, to begin to engage senior managers from core health and local authority children's services. The project was awarded funding from an integration bursary through the Cumbria Partnership Foundation Trust, which allowed us to begin this process. Engaging stakeholders began with identifying and building a relationship with key supporters based in the community, who could use their relationships with others in their organisations to highlight the work that we were doing. A broad spectrum of supporters at all levels emerged, with a common goal: a wish to improve services for families in Barrow. This enabled us to gain further funding from our colleagues in the local authority children's services, including funding for an independent evaluation of Love Barrow Families. The funding from children's services was sourced from the national Troubled Families programme; a large percentage of the families identified in Love Barrow Families also meet the current Troubled Families criteria. Those who did not do so were families who had other significant difficulties, such as long-term parental mental health problems, physical health problems or drug and alcohol misuse. Many of the referrals came from head teachers of local primary schools, who were easily able to identify children already on the pathway to antisocial behaviour and significant emotional difficulties. Love Barrow Families was seized within the community as an opportunity to prevent problems at an early stage.

Core approaches to service in Love Barrow Families

The outcome of this extensive process of family and professional engagement was Love Barrow Families, which had six core components:

- Reorganisation of mainstream services to co-locate a team of workers from the local authority's children's services, adult social care, child and adolescent mental health and adult mental health services, thus bringing adult and children's agencies together (cf. Crittenden, 1992) into a wraparound service that 'thinks family' (C4EO, 2011). Joint working arrangements were put in place through commissioning, with a specification, partnership framework and contract that contributed to the joint approach of the Cumbria Partnership Foundation Trust and Cumbria County Council. Working effectively in a multi-agency model helped ensure families received more coordinated and effective services, and also ensured best value from limited public funds.

- One main key worker for each family who functioned as a 'transitional attachment figure' (Crittenden, 2008) for family members, coordinating all other services and maintaining contact with the family. A transitional attachment figure was someone held in affection and trusted by a family, who could be honest with them about what was needed in order to ensure needs were met. The key worker was, as such, someone who was able to stand in the shoes of parents, providing practical and emotional support tailored to the needs of those particular parents until they began to be able to do this for themselves. Furthermore, having one single keyworker meant that families who were already chaotic themselves did not experience the added chaos which could be caused by multiple agencies, all of which might be well intentioned but arrive with different agendas and assessments.

- One comprehensive assessment that included the AAI and SAA; this assessment encompassed the social and emotional/ mental health needs of both children and parents, rather than separating them. Having one assessment meant that families did not have to tell their story repeatedly to different people and also crucially informed how the whole team worked together to achieve the best outcomes.

- A functional formulation, i.e. an understanding of the function of behaviour for family members within their family, their wider context and the professional system. This included identification of the dangers each family currently experienced, as well as the 'critical causes' of potential change, i.e., the crucial actions for professionals to take (Crittenden & Ainsworth, 1989). Thus the AAIs and the SAA, along with all of the other information provided by families, led to a detailed understanding of why the parents and children in each family behaved in the way they did and was a guide as to which problems caused the most difficulty, which problems could be tackled first and how to go about addressing them in a way which could be shared with the family and was supportive of their strengths. Having such an understanding, which all team members shared and carried in their minds, meant that the family experienced an approach that was cohesive and consistent as well as empathic.

- A community Timebank, which supported families – but also harnessed their assets or skills so that they could give something back. Timebanking is a means of exchange where time is the principal currency. For every hour participant's 'deposit' in a Timebank, perhaps by giving practical help and support to others, they are able to 'withdraw' equivalent support when they themselves are in need (Timebanking UK, 2011). This meant that all families were seen as having something valuable to contribute and were also connected with others in Love Barrow Families. Giving and relating are known to affect physical and mental well-being positively (Action for Happiness, 2015). If accessed early enough, timebanking was one way of intervening at a community level prior to problems becoming so big that they required statutory intervention.
- experienced and qualified senior team members who (a) provided clinical supervision and mentorship for the team and (b) chaired regular advisory 'panel' meetings of other relevant professionals for each family, thus supporting team members and expanding their range of skills.

Development phase

During the months following the co-design phase, sustaining innovation has proven a challenge in the context of anxiety following Serious Case Reviews within Cumbria, and the extensive change in the scale and mode of service delivery following austerity cutbacks. The project took longer to establish than had been anticipated, and at times this felt frustrating. We needed to spend time building relationships in order to have a firm foundation. The initial group of families and frontline practitioners had known what they wanted to do and were keen to get on with it. However, at that time, the connection between professionals on the ground and the most senior managers was not yet established. We had not recognised at the outset that, for the pilot to develop and survive, the participatory process that had taken place among frontline professionals, families and the Barrow community also needed to take place with our colleagues in senior management across both the Cumbria Partnership Foundation Trust and Cumbria County Council. This process has been extremely challenging, but exciting for us all.

A good example of this participatory process with senior management was the agreement we were able to reach with Cumbria County Council for a safeguarding social worker to be seconded from work in child protection to contribute to the Love Barrow Families team. This was something requested by families themselves who told us that it would not work for them to have to be passed back to another agency/worker who did not know them if a child protection issue was to arise. It was their view that child protection concerns could be managed safely in a way that allowed them to be addressed day to day, and they said that they felt better when workers were very honest about concerns rather than passing the matter on to someone else. This happened only with the support of senior managers in Cumbria County Council and also the ongoing support of the local child protection manager who works with the Love Barrow Families team to manage any issues that arise. The multi-agency nature of the Love Barrow Families team allows for cross skilling, i.e. professionals from different agencies learning from one another, and it facilitates close working relationships and communication between workers, thus closing the gaps between agencies – a recurring recommendation highlighted by many Serious Case Reviews in the England, including the case of Baby P.

Love Barrow Families in Action

Starting in January 2014 we began to work with the first cohort of identified families from the two most deprived wards in Barrow, 'growing' our team along the way. The Love Barrow Families team now consists of a project lead, a child and family social worker, a child and family worker, a community support worker for adult mental health and a care coordinator from adult mental health. We also have a social work student in her final year of training. The team is supported by a group of six 'Barrow buddies', volunteers who are matched with families to provide assistance as and when needed. From the beginning we have tried to build on local connections and assets: for example, we appreciate the generosity of Brisbane Park Infant School in providing us with an office that we have made home. The team is governed by a local project board made up of members from a number of agencies, third-sector organisations and Barrow Borough Council. This is important because it supports the work of the team in being true to the underlying principles of the project and the need not to lose sight of our place within our community. We also have a senior executive steering group, which oversees the work of the project and ensures we are properly embedded in the appropriate reporting structures of Cumbria County Council and Cumbria Partnership Foundation Trust. Two of the parents receiving services from Love Barrow Families join us on the project board and steering group. We have recently been visited by the National Troubled Families team and regularly welcome visitors from Cumbria County Council and Cumbria Partnership Foundation Trust.

The team also have the support of a data analyst provided by Cumbria Partnership Foundation Trust, who is assisting with the gathering of data through a weekly report completed with families. As well as this regular report, an outcomes questionnaire has been developed based on the original five top priorities identified by families, thus measuring whether families feel we are doing what we set out to achieve. Cumbria Partnership Foundation Trust has provided the team access to iPads, which are given to families each week so that they can complete the report and the questionnaire themselves. This data will inform family dashboards to give us a sense of how families are getting on, and also to feed into an independent evaluation of our project, which is being undertaken by Northumbria University.

Given the need for the work with stakeholders and the length of time it took to begin to work directly with families, one of our anxieties was that funding would not enable the completion of the two-year pilot and evaluation. In early 2013, we began a conversation with the LankellyChase Foundation, which has the fundamental goal of helping to shift the way that people on the extreme margins are valued by society, so that policy, public debate and practice are focused on people's capabilities and humanity. Talking with the LankellyChase Foundation led to an application for assistance with further funding. Very recently, an agreement has been reached for LankellyChase to provide enough funding to enable us to complete the full two year pilot. This relationship with the LankellyChase Foundation has also allowed us to link with other like-minded projects throughout the country and share learning with them.

We are continuing to develop ways of ensuring that the families we work with feel connected to Love Barrow Families and to the community of Barrow-in-Furness and to make the best use of ideas and answers that they themselves have. Since 2013, we have been very aware of the isolation that families feel and the sense of acceptance and belonging that Love Barrow Families provides. Coming together as a group has been important and we have done this through links with other local projects and groups – such as taking part in community walks and using local facilities such as the Green Heart Den – a green space in the middle of the town centre where parents and children have enjoyed art activities and bug hunting. The parents in our project have recently decided to meet together every two weeks and are keen to assist in organising events which bring everyone together. Thus, some of our families who have benefited from the support provided are now in a position to provide help themselves.

Case Study – the Brown Family

One example of a family who are being worked with within the Love Barrow Families pilot is the Brown family (a pseudonym). They came to Love Barrow Families at a point of serious crisis, when one of the children had been removed and taken into care as a result of his aggressive and threatening behaviour towards Donna (his mother) and his siblings. The AAI was completed with Donna, and SAAs were conducted with each of the three children. The AAI revealed a history of significant and overwhelming trauma and abuse, Donna having been removed herself as a child. The way in which she appeared to have coped was by psychologically escaping from her childhood, i.e. disconnecting from her feelings and, in her own words, 'putting things into boxes'. The AAI helped the team to see how terrifying it was for Donna when her son became aggressive and to understand what meaning this had for her. Not only did the behaviour trigger memories of past abuse at the hands of her father and partners but also Donna had no way of being equipped or able to think about it because keeping these memories locked away had been the way she had managed to survive. When her son became aggressive, Donna became submissive, which was frightening for the son himself and his siblings. The situation ultimately resulted in Donna calling the police in response to a violent incident, and her son being removed for his own and their safety.

Understanding all of this has been crucial to deciding how to proceed with this family. In the first instance, because of Donna's fragility, we talked with her about her strengths and the things that she feels good about. This sounds simple but had a big impact on Donna, who had felt judged and blamed in her previous encounters with professionals. Over a short period of time we provided one-to-one adult attachment work, which aimed at assisting Donna to feel more stable, before beginning the more painful and slow work of supporting her to 'open the boxes' so she could begin to see that, in reality, her little boy did not present the same threat as had her father and others. In the past, Donna had been directed by professionals to a number of parenting courses. She recently commented to us that she had been disappointed in these courses because she always felt as though she was being asked to do things that did not fit her family. However, the co-production ethic of Love Barrow Families meant that she has been able to feel heard within the intervention provided, and she reported that it has been attentive to her needs and those of her children. She also told us:

> I am starting to see things differently than before because I am accepted just as I am by the Love Barrow Families team. I feel like, if they can accept me, then maybe I can accept myself. In Love Barrow Families we all help each other and even though I know I am still struggling I know I am not on my own.

This coming together of the DMM assessments alongside co-production principles meant that the team constantly discussed and analysed the work, including the day-to-day interactions with Donna and her children. Having an understanding of Donna's attachment strategies meant that we have been able to work together with a strong and shared sense of what she can manage, moving one small step at a time. Having workers in our team who see the family every day meant that intensive and practical hands-on support can be provided and then thought about in the context of the wider plan and 'functional formulation'.

Conclusion

At the beginning of our journey we set out to ensure that Love Barrow Families was underpinned by co-production principles and we made every effort to include local families, seeking their view of services and what they felt would be effective. Involving people in partnership with professionals was itself understood to have the potential for beneficial effects, such as being a way of harnessing hidden resources which would otherwise be missed (Boyle and Harris, 2009). Co-production provided a challenge for the way that services were currently set up and delivered, but we anticipated that it could have huge benefits in terms of shaping an intervention, which could occur early and effectively. This helped families to access resources and receive support within their communities, thereby preventing them from coming to the attention of statutory services.

In 2014, co-production principles went from informing the design of the project to shaping the way that we work together in practice with families referred to our team. We strive to reflect that we do not have all the answers, that families themselves equally have skills and wisdom and that, although they may benefit from our experience and training, we need to come together in an equal partnership if change is to be effective and sustained. Remaining true to this is a significant challenge, and team members have an agreement that allows them to challenge themselves and one anther when needed. This way of working is not static; it is a constant process of learning and adapting what we do and how we work to each unique family who comes through our door. Families themselves appear to be proud to be a part of the pilot and have been involved in an extensive reciprocal process of feedback and change.

We started this chapter by highlighting the significance of both the co-production model and the DMM. Love Barrow Families are a team of adult and child mental health and social care workers who are pooling their knowledge and skills so that rather than completing separate assessments for children and parents, they bring this together so that they assess the whole family. The DMM assessments are being used as a way of understanding the function of behaviour for individuals and the meaning for the family. Thus, the psychological understanding of each family, provided by the AAI and SAAs, is shared with the whole team by the therapist who has undertaken them and is used to inform the day-to-day work for all team members in addition to any therapy that is provided. Furthermore, this understanding is used at multi-agency meetings, informing the work of colleagues outside Love Barrow Families. Families are understood within their environment and any practical needs are addressed either before or alongside other support.

In terms of outcomes it is early days for the project as yet and we are mindful of the time needed to ensure fundamental change that will be sustained, particularly when taking into account the impact of multiple disadvantage. The approach that we are taking is developmental and joins up adult and child mental health and social services. As a result, children who are on a pathway to mental health and emotional problems, and their parents, can be given the right help at the earliest stage before patterns become entrenched and become a core part of the family's mode of inter-action. We are hopeful that children, such as Donna's son, benefit from the changes that their parents are able to make, and that this will free them to develop different ways of responding to others – including when they become parents themselves.

Alongside this, we continue to work with our partner organisations locally, ena-bling families who have felt excluded from and isolated within the community of Barrow-in-Furness to begin to develop a sense of belonging to our project. We are building on our connections with the many resources already present in the community, and families are beginning to take part in activities and events that involve them giving of themselves and also connecting with their neighbourhood.

CHAPTER 8

Families as enablers of change: The family by family programme in Australia

Dana Shen, Karen Lewis, Lauren Simpson, Danielle Madsen, Leanne Evans, Fiona Arney and Gill Westhorp

Introduction

The Family by Family (FbyF) model was developed and implemented as one response to the growing demand on the child protection system. This was The Australian Centre for Social Innovation's (TACSI) first service solution to came about after the establishment of this organisation. TACSI was set up following a recommendation by Geoff Mulgan, who had been invited to South Australia as part of the Adelaide Thinkers in Residence programme (Mulgan, 2008).

TACSI draws on the disciplines of design, social science and business to develop and spread solutions, and it assists people and organisations in their ability to innovate. A core tool applied in developing new solutions is co-design. In its simplest form, this means that one develops a set of educated guesses or hunches about what might work, based on multiple forms of evidence. This evidence includes lived experience, practice wisdom, research and theory, and then goes out into the world to test and refine those hunches using methods such as contextual user research, ethnography and prototyping. In relation to FbyF, this meant working closely with the end users – the families – and developing the programme from the ground up (Schulman *et al.*, 2011):

> I had always believed I was very good at listening and understanding the complexity of issues faced by families. Ethnography taught me the importance of listening with more than just your ears. Walking in the shoes of a family provided experiential learning that could never be communicated in a more formal interaction. (family coach)

FbyF set out with the vision 'to see all Australian families thrive, not just survive' (see www.tacsi.org.au/solutions/family-by-family/; accessed 20 January 2015). Thriving families move towards what they want, they try new things, plan for the future, connect family members to new opportunities and offer positive feedback and mutual support. They are less likely to require future government support services and are less likely to have children removed from the home and placed into state care.

This chapter will provide a 'deep dive' into the model to explore the nuance of the practice ('deep dive' is a term to explain going beneath the surface of a story or issue, exploring deeper into the reasons why or the argument behind it). It will focus on how the programme: builds relationships between families; is professionally supported; and seeks to expand the impact and involvement of children and young people in creating change for other families. Though much has remained consistent over time, the staff and families who have contributed to FbyF have helped the organisation better understand and adapt the model for families as it scales out.

The Family by Family programme

FbyF is a peer-to-peer support programme that brings together two types of families. The first – Sharing Families – are families who have been through difficult and challenging times but have come out the other side and are willing to share their experiences with another family. The second type – Seeking Families – are families that are going through difficult or challenging times and are wanting to change something in their lives.

FbyF brings together Sharing and Seeking Families in what is called a link-up. A link-up can last 10–30 weeks and focuses on setting goals and improving these over time. Both families are supported by a professional family coach, who often takes an indirect role, motivating, prompting and problem-solving, rather than assessing, diagnosing or directing change.

Change is created by:

- increasing a family's sense of choice and control;
- strengthening attachment between parents and children;
- enabling behaviour modelling through families learning from each other;
- facilitating goal setting, accountability and reflection between families;
- increasing reciprocity between families.

Recruiting families

FbyF does not ask the question: 'Who is eligible for FbyF?', but rather: 'Who is attracted to FbyF?' This results in grouping families in terms of their motivations and goals instead of their professionally assessed risks or needs. The four types of Seeking Families attracted to FbyF are: families who are stuck; families in and out of crisis; families moving on after a crisis; and families wanting more help (Schulman *et al.*, 2011). It is useful to remember this when thinking about how to engage with families, as it is in language that families can understand and it recognises the potential of families to change their lives and assist others. Because FbyF is a voluntary programme, the only eligibility criteria for Seeking Families is that they have children under eighteen years in the home and that they are wanting to make change in their lives.

Families can self-refer into the programme as well as be referred by other people and organisations who work with families. Over time, FbyF has found that self-referral is quite a common way in which families will become part of the programme.

FbyF also takes an assertive role to encourage family participation by ensuring the programme is visible and accessible within local communities. All efforts are made to create and attend events, sites and activities where families visit and are involved. This could include barbecues, playgrounds, childcare centres and shopping centres.

This proactive approach to finding potential Sharing and Seeking Families is intended to track down not only those who are currently or have previously been involved with services, but also those who may have not been involved with services but still require support. Recruitment in this fashion also provides an opportunity for families to opt into a programme themselves rather than feeling the pressure of a worker who has told them to be involved.

The Sharing Family
Potential Sharing Families go through two stages of assessment and training. The first is a Sharing Family dinner with all members of the potential Sharing Family, including the children. This interaction is an opportunity for the family to learn more about FbyF and for the family coaches to identify the family's strengths and how they could contribute to the programme.

The Sharing Family dinner is carried out in a family-friendly way that includes the family game as well as a children's book to explain the model to children and the adults in the family. The family game has been specifically designed to help identify a set of thriving behaviours that the programme would ideally like in a potential Sharing Family. The family coaches also provide the meal (often a takeaway treat) in order to create the most natural environment for coaches and families to get to know each other.

The second stage is Sharing Family training. This has been provided in two different forms: a residential two-day camp; and two separate training days. Training covers more detailed information about FbyF, the expectations in relation to what is required from their family as well as fun exercises and activities for the whole family.

The primary role of a Sharing Family is connecting with other families, their children and community. Providing training to groups of potential Sharing Families allows the family coaches to observe in a more candid way how families relate to their children, to each other and how they interact with other families:

> FbyF has brought our family closer together, working together for a greater cause. I get a sense of satisfaction and a sense of achievement out of FbyF. It has turned my hardship into a worthwhile tool and my kids have developed a level of empathy I could not of ever imagined. (Sharing Family)

The Seeking Family

Following an initial telephone discussion, the family coach will meet the Seeking Family, most often in their home. The FbyF programme is explained and, if the family wishes to proceed, they are shown a number of Sharing Family profiles to choose from – these having been filtered by the family coach according to their availability, capacity and the appropriateness for this Seeking Family.

The Seeking Family is empowered by selecting their Sharing Family rather than having one allocated to them. Seeking Families seem to opt for Sharing Families based on the journey the Sharing Family has been through, the number and age of children in the family and also the shared values between both families.

The next stage is a Meet and Greet between the Seeking Family, the family coach and the Sharing Family. As well as starting the getting-to-know-you process, this meeting is an opportunity to formalise agreements between the two families and discuss the purpose and aims of the link-up.

To help families identify their goals, FbyF developed a goal-setting tool called the Bubbles. The Seeking Family chooses one particular thing they really want to see change, identifies the steps they will take to achieve this and what they expect to happen if their goals are gained.

By setting the goals at the Meet and Greet with both families present, the Seeking Family is empowered by deciding what it is they want to work on, the family coach can make a decision on the likely length of the link-up and the two families can build their relationship.

FbyF has found that the sooner the family coach can leave this initial interaction the better for the families involved. One new family coach explained:

> It was my first time involved in a Meet and Greet. My role, as I understood it, was to introduce the families and go through the formalities and consent forms. I found as the meeting went along and the paperwork had been completed that my role became less important. The Seeking and Sharing Families were discussing the lives of their children and what was important to them, and, despite my trying to comment and be part of the discussion, I realised no one was actually listening to me; I was no longer important in the connection between these two families. This was initially challenging as I have not been used to being ignored in a professional setting. I then realised what this model was all about – it is the relationship between two families. I quickly left the meeting.

The Link-up Journey

The journey through FbyF is based on the relationship between the three main players: Sharing Family, Seeking Family and the family coach. In order to achieve the Seeking Family's goals, the journey of the Seeking and Sharing Family is based on a three-stage process.

The first is the relationship stage, during which the Sharing and Seeking Families take the time needed to develop and build a trusting relationship. This step is vital to the success of the link-up and may need to be returned to at different points of the link-up journey:

> It's often a bit nerve wracking and you get anxious about first meeting your new Seeking Family, but then you sit down over a cup of tea, start chatting and, before you realise it, the time has just disappeared. Great mates are born over cups of tea. (Sharing Family)

> Lots of people are in that bit where they are trying to get through it but they can't get out the other side so you can go, you know what, I did this; I've been here; I've done that. I can help you get out the other side. It can be done. It's not a completely hopeless situation. (Sharing Family)

The second stage is 'Doing With'. In this, the families look at the goals that the Seeking Family wants to achieve and together spend time working on these. During this stage, the Sharing Family 'walks' alongside the Seeking Family, showing how – rather than telling – and celebrating small wins and achievements.

Encouragement from another family (not a professional) appears to play an important role in a Seeking Family's ability to create change. For a Seeking Family, it is good to connect with another family who has probably been through a similar, if not the same, situation, where they are not judged and where the creation of behaviour change is normalised through everyday interactions between people in the community:

> I don't know if it's like this for every family, it's more than just support, we're good friends. I can call Sophie about anything. This link-up has been a really good match, we're really connected. It's a good support network to lean on when we need help. (Seeking Family)

The third stage, 'Doing Without', is when the Sharing Family continues to support the Seeking Family but starts to back away and reduce their involvement. The Seeking Family is encouraged to work towards their goals and practise what they have learnt by themselves. An important part of the FbyF model is to enhance resilience and extend support networks rather than generate dependency.

This transition is not always easy for a Seeking Family. Often the goals faced by them can be some of the most challenging things in their lives. This final phase must be handled with a gentle approach where the Sharing Family is strategic in how they support the Seeking Family to make change. For example, a Sharing Family was supporting a Seeking Family to return to education. Initially, the Sharing Family attended classes with the Seeking Family. Nearing the end of the link-up, the Sharing Family would meet the family at the class, but leave them at the door and follow up later to see that they had attended the classes, providing support and encouragement.

Case Study – Stephanie

Stephanie approached us at a parent's group and asked: 'Could you help me? Child Protection think I neglect my kids?' Stephanie shared with us that she had a number of notifications made against her in the past year and that she was being taken to court (notifications are reports made to the Australian Child Protection Authority when child abuse or neglect is suspected within a family). When asked if she struggled to clothe or feed her children, she replied: 'No, but I would like to learn how to love them!'

After a conversation with her case manager we were told the Child Protection Authority was planning to remove all four children from Stephanie's care. A six-month order was granted for the family to try the FbyF programme.

Stephanie had four children:

❑ Angus (thirteen), who was responsible for all cleaning, cooking and nappy changes in the home. Angus was in constant trouble at school and often suspended;

❑ Bianca (seven), who made routine phone calls to child protection asking for a new family — as a result, she was blamed by mum for their troubles;

❑ Leon (five) was still in nappies and would sit in his own waste during school because teachers would not take responsibility;

❑ Tammy (two) would sit silently in her pram for hours, showed developmental delay in talking and walking and would pull herself around with her arms.

FbyF introduced Stephanie to John and Ally. Together the two families discussed the changes Stephanie wanted to make, quickly developing a trusting relationship.

They had a barbecue together and Stephanie learnt how to play football. Angus commented: 'It is nice to see mum play with us, I couldn't believe it when she kicked the footy.' They went on days out where they practised praising children and a camping trip where the Sharing Family modelled adult roles versus child roles.

The camping trip was a turning point for the two families. As it was an overnight stay, the Sharing Family were able to witness Tammy crying during the night with no response from mum. They asked the simple question: 'Do you think she feels scared?' and modelled a comforting response. This was when the penny dropped for Stephanie, commenting to her family coach: 'I didn't know that this is what they meant by neglect.'

Through thirty weekly interactions, Stephanie started putting ideas into practice at home, realising it was her job to make her family feel safe. Although at first Stephanie commented that it felt unnatural, she also began giving her children cuddles.

The two families attended school and agency meetings together and set up routines in the house. The Sharing Family suggested toilet training tips for Leon, spending time in the home practising new techniques. Within two months, Leon no longer required nappies.

Bianca, as part of the new routine, received one-on-one mummy time, resulting in child protection no longer receiving phone calls. Tammy started talking during one of their camping trips and not only began to walk, but also to run — something that surprised disability services involved.

Stephanie felt she had a more concrete understanding of her role in the family and stopped placing blame on the children, instead taking a lead in putting boundaries in place. During the last weeks of the link-up, the Sharing Family set Stephanie challenges to try without them and celebrated when she did these things on her own.

The Child Protection Authority commented that they have never seen such a quick turn around in a family before, and believed that it was due to the in-context learning Stephanie had been exposed to, something they could not provide. Six months later, Stephanie's case was completely closed.

The Ongoing Journey

It is assumed and understood that Sharing Families, at some times in their lives, may run into their own life challenges. If this occurs, the Sharing Family will be supported to maintain their involvement or take a break for a while from link-ups. At times, Sharing Families have become Seeking Families and sought help through a link-up from another Sharing Family.

This supports the general premise of the FbyF programme that all families at one point or another can be both Sharing and Seeking Families, and it acknowledges that all families have ups and downs.

The values and developing principles of FbyF is further enhanced by the fact a number of Seeking Families have also gone on to become Sharing Families. One Sharing Family explained:

Becoming a Sharing Family has changed the way I think. When I was a Seeking Family my mindset was: 'How can I get help to solve this or that problem in our family?' Now I think as a Sharing Family. The frequent questions in my mind are: 'What can I do to help my link-up family?' and 'What are the things they can do to help themselves?'

After becoming a Sharing Family, the more families I meet, the more compassionate I become. Every family is different and unique. People have the right to live the life they want to live and I appreciate their courage. Every family is inspiring, no matter their shape, culture or experience.

Measuring Change for Families

Just like the FbyF programme itself, the process of measurement and evaluation was co-designed and developed in partnership with families, with the aim of assessing change in a way that was family-friendly and easy to understand. As stated earlier in this chapter, this process is started when families first meet each other. At the beginning of the link-up, the Seeking Family is asked to rate how they feel about each of their goals. This question is raised again at joint coaching sessions at week five, ten, twenty or thirty weeks, depending on the length of the link-up.

Joint coaching sessions with the Seeking Family and Sharing Family are an opportunity for the family coach to ensure the goals set at the beginning are still relevant, the families are keeping on track and that movement is being made towards achieving those goals. Goals can be modified if required or changed entirely at joint coaching meetings.

Final ratings are taken at the end of the link-up. The Seeking Family is shown their initial goal rating so they can compare how far they have come. The end of link-up is a time for celebration for both families. Some families will continue their connection and friendship, while others move on – thankful for the time spent together.

The family coach: The professional in the background

As emphasised in the previous sections, the relationship between Seeking and Sharing Family is the most significant element of the

FbyF model. The level of involvement in the relationship between the Seeking and Sharing Family varies depending on the stage of the link-up journey, the needs of the Seeking Family or the support requirements of the Sharing Family. Another important person is the family coach. Family coaches are the professionals in the background, or in the back seat. They can have diverse professional experiences including as educators, life coaches and social workers.

A key role of the family coach is maintaining the relationship between the Sharing and Seeking Family. The family coach helps the Sharing Family to support the Seeking Family and intervenes only where required: for example, where there are more complex issues or ongoing child protection issues. Family coaches facilitate weekly sessions with small groups of Sharing Families to develop their skills through training and guest speakers. Weekly coaching is also when Sharing Families discuss their link-ups, talk about their experiences, what they are learning and where they are finding things challenging. Coaching allows families to contribute and supporting each other and is one of the main avenues the family coach can provide advice and help.

A challenging and important skill for a family coach is that of understanding when to be more forward in the relationship between the Seeking and Sharing Family and when to stay more in the back seat. A family coach explained:

> While working as a family coach I have been inspired by Sharing Families and their skills, surprised by how humble they are and how strong they can be when they are confronted by adversity. More often I'm very much in the background, then there are other times when it is important to lead them and encourage them with knowledge and patience. All families have times when they feel vulnerable but what makes a Sharing Family different is how they pick themselves up. My role is to show them how to use skills they have developed over the years as great tools to create better families.

Engaging Children as Change-makers

Although FbyF maintains a focus on the family unit rather than the individuals within families, over time the programme has increasingly recognised the invaluable, and often underestimated, role that children play in creating change for others. In order to understand more about how the programme could better engage and support children as change-makers, FbyF involved children in a research project that followed the co-design process.

Ethnographic work and specifically created co-design tools for children were used to gain insights, opportunities and barriers around children as change-makers within the programme. The research concluded that there are four critical areas that need to be considered in order to enable children to create change with and for others.

Play

Being a biological drive, play is the primary mechanism through which children explore their immediate world. Perhaps, unsurprisingly, when children involved in FbyF were asked about what they thought their role in link-ups should be, they overwhelmingly answered 'to play'. Children's strong drive and desire to play is often overlooked as trivial. However, play has many benefits for individuals and the communities they live in.

Research suggests that play is vital for cognitive, creative, emotional, physical and social development, and these benefits last through adulthood (Brown and Patte, 2013). Just as importantly, particularly in EI programmes such as FbyF, play also provides opportunities for families to connect with each other, strengthening parent–child relationships.

> Heather (three) would often play peek-a-boo with the baby in the family we were linked up with. The mum and baby didn't play many games together but Heather seemed to encourage more fun and play between them. (Sharing Family)

Voice

Throughout the project, children made it clear that they were often underestimated by adults. The factors that appeared to obstruct children's voice and participation in link-ups included attitudes and behaviours of the coaches and parents leading a link-up, as well as a lack of resources and tools within the programme that encouraged child involvement. In link-ups where efforts were made to foster children's participation, the benefits included:

- opportunities for children to develop life skills such as empathy and cooperation;
- children developing and expressing gratitude;
- an increase in children's confidence;
- more opportunities to role model positive family interactions;
- increasing children's skills in decision-making;
- strengthened parent–child relationships;
- greater engagement of the whole family in the link-up.

The next steps were to revisit the main interaction points of the FbyF programme (e.g. first meeting with a family to explain the programme) and consider how the engagement and participation of children might be further encouraged.

> How come we never get to decide where we could go on link-ups? I have some good ideas about that you know. (Sharing Child, aged seven)

Role modelling

When co-designing the FbyF programme, families described learning by doing, yet there were few opportunities for whole families to see and try new ways of doing. Observing children of all ages in interactions with their parents has proved to be a powerful mechanism for change.

The inclusion of children and young people in role modelling positive family interactions may also help to build a perception of similarity between families, which, in turn, increases the effectiveness of the role modelling. In other words, parents watch and learn from other parents who are experiencing similar stages and challenges of parenthood but can show different and sometimes helpful ways of interacting with their children:

> My daughter and I were singing nursery rhymes in the car with our Seeking Family. I noticed that our Seeking

Family's daughter didn't know any of the rhymes and was copying my daughter. (Sharing Family)

Support

Reflections from children demonstrated that involvement in link-ups provided them with opportunities to develop important life skills. According to the World Health Organization, life skills may be defined as: 'abilities for adaptive and positive behaviour, that enable individuals to deal effectively with the demands and challenges of everyday life' (WHO, 1997). Uniquely, the FbyF programme allowed children to practise applying developing life skills in real situations but with the back-up of other children involved in the programme as well as parents and coaches. Notably, parents reported that the skills their children had learnt from link-ups had helped them to tackle challenges in other parts of their life, such as school and online, more effectively:

> I'd like to help Max when he gets so angry but I'm just not sure what to do. (Sharing Child, aged thirteen)

> Through FbyF our kids are learning skills that will help them as teenagers and beyond. Our kids are future leaders! (Sharing Mum)

Conclusion

Given some promising results in an evaluation report released in 2012 (Westhorp, 2012), the FbyF programme is now planning to be trialled in several states in Australia and is looking for opportunities internationally. Furthermore, efforts are being made to develop the rigour and depth in which the programme is evaluated over time.

FbyF is currently expanding in South Australia and also has a site in Mount Druitt, Western Sydney. As part of its introduction of new places, TACSI is implementing and developing a scoping approach for any new site. Scoping is the method for understanding the local community and service system in order to ensure that the model is adapted for local families and that it works in partnership with local services.

Two scoping reports have now been completed: the first in Playford (the northern metropolitan area in Adelaide) and the second (TACSI, 2013) in Mount Druitt (western Sydney). In describing their experience, one family coach stated:

> I met with the family I had previously worked with for three years, and I must say I now know more about them all after spending a few hours with them using these tools during scoping than I did

in all the years before. Families told us they are excited about FbyF and many want to be involved as either Seeking or Sharing Families (TACSI, 2013).

In addition, TACSI has committed to developing its own response to Indigenous Australians and is working to develop the FbyF programme as a programme of choice. TACSI believes that, when Indigenous families feel they can self-refer into the programme, it will have achieved an important milestone.

Through a dedicated family strategy, TACSI is also seeking to have a broader social impact in addition to the FbyF programme. The strategy will consider how families in general can have a bigger role in influencing the broader social services system and improving outcomes for other families. It will also consider how FbyF could be more broadly adapted and scaled in order to inform other programme and policy areas. Furthermore, it is considering how to support the social service system to use the co-design process to improve outcomes for children and families. Finally, TACSI aims to build the capability of organisations to become more adaptive systems.

These are ambitious goals, but, as TACSI's main aim is to demonstrate the broadest positive impact for the community, the hope is that the FbyF programme can be used as a lever to encourage greater social and system change.

REFERENCES

Action for Children (n.d.) 'Early intervention: Where now for local authorities?' (online). Available from URL: www.actionforchildren.org.uk/media/5740124/afc_early_intervention_-_final.pdf (accessed 5 February 2015)

Action for Happiness (2015) '10 keys to happier living' (online). Available from URL: www.actionforhappiness.org/10-keys-to-happier-living (accessed 19 February 2015)

Aldgate, J. (2010) 'Child well-being, child development and family life', in McAuley, C. and Rose, W. (eds) (2010) *Child Well-Being: Understanding Children's Lives*, London: Jessica Kingsley

Allen, G. (2011) *Early Intervention: The Next Steps*, an independent report to Her Majesty's Government, London: Cabinet Office

Allen, G. and Duncan Smith, I. (2010) 'The cross-party challenge: Early intervention for children and families', *Journal of Children's Services*, Vol. 5, No. 1, pp. 4–8

Angus Local Community Council (2013) 'Getting it right for every child: Measuring outcomes in Angus' (online). Available from URL: www.angus.gov.uk/girfec (accessed 20 January 2015)

Barnsdale, L. and Walker, M. (2007) *Examining the Use and Impact of Family Group Conferencing*, Edinburgh: Scottish Executive

Batty, E. and Flint, J. (2013) 'Talking 'bout poor folks (thinking 'bout my folks): Perspectives on comparative poverty in working class households', *International Journal of Housing Policy*, Vol. 13, No. 1, pp. 1–19

BBC (2011) 'Many children's centres "under threat of closure"' (online). Available from URL: www.bbc.co.uk/news/education-12182994 (accessed 20 January 2015)

BBC (2013) 'Social workers under "phenomenal pressure"' (online). Available from URL: www.bbc.co.uk/news/education-24999826 (accessed 20 January 2015)

Best, T. and Wilson, M. (2007) 'Northern Ireland', in Ashley, C. and Nixon, P. (eds) (2007) *Family Group Conferences – Where Next? Policies and Practices for the Future*, London: Family Rights Group, pp. 229–35

Birmingham City Council (2014) 'Review of early years, children's centres & family support' (online). Available from URL: www.birmingham.gov.uk/cs/Satellite/earlyyearsreview?packedargs=website%3D4&rendermode=live (accessed 5 February 2015)

Boyle, D. and Harris, M. (2009) *The Challenge of Co-Production*, London: Nesta

Brandon, M., Howe, D., Black, J. and Dodsworth, J. (2002) *Learning How to Make Children Safer Part 2: An Analysis for the Welsh Office of Serious Child Abuse Cases in Wales*, Norwich: University of East Anglia/Welsh Office

Breuer, J. T. (1999) *The Myth of the First Three Years*, New York: The Free Press

Brewer, M. and Shephard, A. (2004) *Has Labour Made Work Pay?*, York: Joseph Rowntree Foundation. Available from URL: www.jrf.org.uk/sites/files/jrf/1859352626.pdf (accessed 5 February 2015)

Broadhurst, K., Doherty, P., Yeend, E., Holt, K. and Kelly, N. (2013) *Coventry and Warwickshire Pre-Proceedings Pilot: Final Research Report*, Lancaster and Bradford: Lancaster University and Bradford University. Available from URL: www.bradford.ac.uk/ssis/media/ssis/socialwork/Coventry-and-Warwickshire.-Pre-Proceedings-Pilot.pdf (accessed 5 February 2015)

Brooks-Gunn, J., Schneider, W. and Waldfogel, J. (2012) 'The great recession and the risk of child maltreatment', *Child Abuse and Neglect*, Vol. 37, No. 10, pp. 721–9

Brown, F. and Patte, M. (2013) *Rethinking Children's Play*, London: Bloomsbury Academic

Buckley, H. and O'Nolan, C. (2013) *An Examination of Recommendations from Inquiries into Events in Families and Their Interactions with State Services, and Their Impact on Policy and Practice*, Dublin: Department of Children and Youth Affairs and Irish Research Council Publication

Butler, I. (2011) 'Children's policy in Wales', in Williams, C. (ed.) (2011) *Social Policy for Social Welfare Practice in a Devolved Wales*, Birmingham: Venture

Butler, P. (2014) 'Birmingham city council leader warns of "ticking time-bomb" of financial cuts' (online). Available from URL: www.theguardian.com/society/2014/sep/16/birmingham-city-council-leader-ticking-time-bomb-financial-cuts (accessed 5 February 2015)

C4EO (2010) *Grasping the Nettle, Early Intervention for Children, Communities and Families*, London: Centre for Excellence and Outcomes in Children and Young People's Services

C4EO (2011) *Improving the Health, Safety and Wellbeing of Children*, London: Centre for Excellence and Outcomes in Children and Young People's Services

Cameron, D. (2011) 'Troubled families speech' delivered 15 December (online). Available at URL: www.gov.uk/government/speeches/troubled-families-speech (accessed 19 February 2015)

Cardy, S. (2013) 'How should social workers support children and families facing destitution and cuts to their benefits?' (online). Available from URL: www.socialworkfuture.org/articles-and-analysis/articles/306-how-should-social-workers-support-children-in-poverty (accessed 5 February 2015)

Carpenter, J., Brown, S, and Griffin, M. (2007) 'Prevention in integrated children's services: The impact of Sure Start on referrals to social services and child protection registrations', *Child Abuse Review*, Vol. 16, No. 1, p. 1

Casey, L. (2012) *Listening to Troubled Families*, London: Troubled Families Unit

Children and Young People Now (2014) 'Troubled families programme on course to miss targets' (online). Available from URL: www.cypnow. co.uk/cyp/news/1143244/troubled-families-programme-set-miss-targets (accessed 19 February 2015)

Children in Scotland (2014) 'Briefing: Children and Young People (Scotland) Bill – Part 4 (Provision of Named Persons)' (online). Available from URL: www.childreninscotland.org.uk (accessed 20 January 2015)

Coen, L., Canavan, J. and Brennan, M. (2012) *Mol an Óige/Family Preservation Final Evaluation Report*, Galway: National University of Ireland, UNESCO Child and Family Research Centre; Mayo and Roscommon: Health Service Executive West, Child and Family Services

Communities and Local Government (2012) *The Troubled Families Programme: Financial Framework for the Troubled Families Programme's Payment by Results Scheme for Local Authorities*, London: Information Policy Team

Cooper, K. and Stewart, K. (2013) *Does Money Affect Children's Outcomes?*, York: Joseph Rowntree Foundation

CPAG (2014) 'Child poverty facts and figures' (online). Available from URL: www.cpag.org.uk/child-poverty-facts-and-figures (accessed 5 February 2015)

Crampton, D. (2007) 'Research review: Family group decision making: A promising practice in need of more programme theory and research', *Child and Family Social Work*, Vol. 12, No. 2, pp. 202–9

Crittenden, P. M. (1992) 'The social ecology of treatment: Case study of a service system for maltreated children', *American Journal of Orthopsychiatry*, Vol. 62, pp. 22–34

Crittenden, P. M. (2008) *Raising Parents: Attachment, Parenting, and Child Safety*, London: Routledge

Crittenden, P. M. and Ainsworth, M. D. S. (1989) 'Child maltreatment and attachment theory', in Cicchetti, D. and Carlson, V. (eds) (1989) *Handbook of Child Maltreatment*, New York: Cambridge University Press, pp. 432–63

Crittenden, P. M., Robson, K. and Tooby, A. (2015, forthcoming) 'Longitudinal, concurrent, and construct validation of the school-age assessment of attachment', *Clinical Child Psychology and Psychiatry*

Cross, S., Hubbard, A. and Munro, E. (2010) *Reclaiming Social Work: London Borough of Hackney Children and Young People's Services*, London: Human Reliability and London School of Economics & Political Science

Crowley, A. (2011) 'Child poverty in Wales: A failed promise?', in Williams, C. (ed.) (2011) *Social Policy for Social Welfare Practice in a Devolved Wales*, Birmingham: Venture

Crozier, L. (2000) 'The evolution of conferencing within child welfare in Northern Ireland', in Burford, G. and Hudson, J. (eds) (2000) *Family Group Conferencing: New Directions in Community-Centred Child and Family Practice*, New York: Aldine de Gruyter, pp. 218–23

Daly, M. (2010) 'Shifts in family policy in the UK under New Labour', *Journal of European Social Policy*, Vol. 20. No. 5, pp. 433–43

Davis, J. M. (2011) *Integrated Children's Services*, London: Sage

Davis, J. M. and Smith, M. (2012) *Working in Multi-Professional Contexts: A Practical Guide for Professionals in Children's Services*, London: Sage

DCLG (2012) *Working with Troubled Families: A Guide to the Evidence and Good Practice*, London: Department for Communities and Local Government. Available from URL: https://www.gov.uk/government/uploads/system/uploads/attachment_data/file/66113/121214_Working_with_troubled_families_FINAL_v2.pdf (accessed 20 January 2015)

DCLG (2013) *The Cost of Troubled Families*, London: Department for Communities and Local Government. Available from URL: http://socialwelfare.bl.uk/subject-areas/services-client-groups/families/departmentforcommunitiesandlocalgovernment/144219The_Cost_of_Troubled_Families_v1.pdf (accessed 20 January 2015)

Department of Health, Department for Education and Employment, and Home Office (2000) *Framework for the Assessment of Children in Need and Their Families*, London: The Stationery Office

DES (2003) *Every Child Matters: Change for Children*, London: The Stationery Office. Available from URL: www.education.gov.uk/consultations/downloadableDocs/EveryChildMatters.pdf (accessed 5 February 2015)

DES (2006) *Care Matters: Transforming the Lives of Children and Young People in Care*, London: Department for Education and Skills

DES (2012) 'The CSAF process' (online). Available from URL: http://webarchive.nationalarchives.gov.uk/20130903161352/www.education.gov.uk/childrenandyoungpeople/strategy/integratedworking/caf/a0068957/the-caf-process (accessed 5 February 2015)

DES (2013) 'Children looked after in England, including adoption' (online). Available from URL: www.gov.uk/government/publications/children-looked-after-in-england-including-adoption (accessed 5 February 2015)

Devaney, C., Canavan, J., Landy, F. and Gillen, A. (2013) *What Works in Family Support?*, Dublin: Child and Family Agency

Devaney, C. and Dolan, P. (2014) 'Voice and meaning: The wisdom of Family Support veterans', *Child & Family Social Work*

Devaney, J., McAndrew, F. and Rodgers, T. (2010) 'Our children and young people – our shared responsibility: The reform implementation process in child protection services in Northern Ireland', in Stafford, A., Vincent, S. and Parton, N. (eds) (2010) *Child Protection Reform Across the UK*, Edinburgh: Dunedin, pp. 45–61

DHSSPS (2007) *Care Matters in Northern Ireland – A Bridge to a Better Future*, Belfast: Department of Health, Social Services and Public Safety

DHSSPS (2009a) *Families Matter: Supporting Families in Northern Ireland – Regional Family and Parenting Strategy*, Belfast: Department of Health, Social Services and Public Safety

DHSSPS (2009b) *Priorities for Action 2009–10*, Belfast: Department of Health, Social Services and Public Safety

DHSSPS (2013) *Children's Social Care Statistics for Northern Ireland 2012/13*, Belfast: Northern Ireland statistics and Research Agency/Department of Health, Social Services and Public Safety

Dillane, J., Hill, M., Bannister, J. and Scott, S. (2001) *Evaluation of the Dundee Families Project*, Edinburgh: Scottish Executive, Dundee City Council, NCH Scotland

Dolan, P. (2006) 'Assessment, intervention and self-appraisal tools for family support', in Dolan, P., Pinkerton, J. and Canavan, J. (eds) (2006) *Family Support as Reflective Practice*, London and Philadelphia: Jessica Kingsley, pp. 196–213

Dolan, P., Peasgood, T. and White, M. P. (2006) *Review of Research on the Influences on Personal Wellbeing and Application to Policy*, London: Department for Environment, Food and Rural Affairs

Dolan, P., Brady, B., O'Regan, C., Russell, D., Canavan, J. and Forkan, C. (2011) *Big Brothers Big Sisters of Ireland: Evaluation Study: Report One: Randomised Controlled Trial and Implementation Report*, Galway: Child and Family Research Centre

Dolan, P. and Brady, B. (2012) *A Guide to Youth Mentoring; Providing Effective Social Support*, London and Philadelphia: Jessica Kingsley

Dolan, P., Smith, B., Smith, M. and Davis, J. (2015) 'Family support and child welfare in Ireland: Capacities and possibilities', in Vincent, S. (ed) (2015) *Early Intervention: Supporting and Strengthening Families*, Edinburgh: Dunedin, Chapter 4

Doughty, S. (2013) '£450m scheme for problem families to turn their lives around helps just 1,500 parents find work' (online). Available from URL: www.dailymail.co.uk/news/article-2513577/450m-scheme-problem-families-turn-lives-helps-just-1–500-parents-work.html?ITO=1490&ns_mchannel=rss&ns_campaign=1490 (accessed 20 January 2015)

Drakeford, M. (2005), 'Wales and a third term of New Labour: Devolution and the development of difference', *Critical Social Policy*, Vol. 25, No. 4, pp. 497–506

Drakeford, M. (2007) 'Social justice in a devolved Wales', *Benefits*, Vol. 15, No. 2, pp. 171–8

Duffy, S. (2014) 'Poverty and welfare reform' (online). Available from URL: www.centreforwelfarereform.org/library/authors/simon-duffy/poverty-and-welfare-reform.html (accessed 5 February 2015)

Duncan Smith, I. and Osborne, G. (2014) 'The Conservative's child poverty plan tackles poverty at source' (online). Available from URL: www.theguardian.com/commentisfree/2014/feb/26/conservative-child-poverty-strategy-george-osborne-iain-Duncan Smith (accessed 5 February 2015)

East Renfrewshire Child Protection Committee (2014) 'Getting it right for every child in East Renfrewshire: Multi-agency summary guidance for practitioners and managers' (online). Available from URL: www.eastrenfrewshire.gov.uk/ercpc (accessed 20 January 2015)

Eisenstadt, N. (2011) *Providing a Sure Start: How Government Discovered Early Childhood*, Bristol: The Policy Press

Featherstone, B., Morris, K. and White, S. (2013) 'A marriage made in hell: Early intervention meets child protection', *British Journal of Social Work*; doi: 10.1093/bjsw/bct052

Featherstone, B., White, S. and Morris, K. (2014) *Re-imagining Child Protection: Towards Humane Social Work with Families*, Bristol: The Policy Press

Ferguson, I. and Lavalette, M. (2009) 'Social work after "Baby P"', *International Socialism: A Quarterly Journal of Socialist Theory*. Available from URL: www.isj.org.uk/index.php4?id=534 (accessed 5 February 2015)

Ferragina, E., Tomlinson, M. and Walker, R. (2013) *Poverty, Participation and Choice: The Legacy of Peter Townsend*, York: Joseph Rowntree Foundation

Field, F. (2010) *The Foundation Years: Preventing Poor Children Becoming Poor Adults*, Report of the Independent Review on Poverty and Life Chances, London: Cabinet Office

Fletcher, A., Gardner, F., McKee, M. and Bonell, C. (2012) 'The British government's troubled families program: A flawed response to riots and youth offending', *BMJ*, 344:e3403, pp. 8–9

Flint, J., Batty, E., Parr, S. *et al.* (2011) *Evaluation of Intensive Intervention Projects*, London: Department for Education

Freitag, M. and Vatter, A. (eds) (2009) *Vergleichende Subnationale Analysen für Deutschland: Institutionen, Staatstätigkeiten und Politische Kulturen*, Berlin: Lit. Verlag

Friedman, M. (2009) 'Turning the curve' (online). Available from URL: www.raguide.org (accessed 20 January 2015)

Frost, N. and Dolan, P. (2012) 'The theoretical foundations of family support work', in Davies, M. (ed.) (2012) *Social Work with Children and Families*, Houndsmill: Palgrave Macmillan

Garrett, P.-M. (2009) *Transforming Children's Services: Social Work, Neo-Liberalism and the 'Modern World'*, Buckingham: Open University Press

Gibbons, N. (2010) *Roscommon Child Care Case, Report of the Inquiry Team to the Health Service Executive*, Dublin: The Stationery Office

Glass, N. (1999) 'Sure Start: The development of an early intervention programme for young children in the United Kingdom', *Children and Society*, Vol. 13, pp. 263 ff.

Glass, N. (2005) 'Surely some mistake?' (online). Available from URL: http://www.theguardian.com/society/2005/jan/05/guardiansocietysupplement.childrensservices (Accessed 5 february 2015)

Gove, M. (2013) 'Getting it right for children in need' (online). Speech to the NSPCC, 12 November 2013. Available from URL: www.gov.uk/government/speeches/getting-it-right-for-children-in-need-speech-to-the-nspcc (accessed 5 February 2015)

Graungaard, A. and Skov, L. (2007) 'Why do we need a diagnosis? A qualitative study of parents' experiences, coping and needs when the newborn child is severely disabled', *Child: Care, Health and Development*, Vol. 33, No. 3, pp. 296–307

Graybeal, C. (2001) 'Strengths-based social work assessment: Transforming the dominant paradigm', *Families in Society*, Vol. 82, No. 3, pp. 233–42

Gunderson, K., Cahn, K. and Wirth, J. (2003) 'The Washington State long-term outcome study', *Protecting Children*, Vol. 18, Nos 1 and 2

Halpenny, A., Greene, S. and Hogan, D. (2008) 'Children's perspectives on coping and support following parental separation', *Child Care in Practice*,

Vol. 14, No. 3, pp. 311–25

Ham, C., Heenan, D., Longley, M. and Steel, D. (2013) *Integrated Care in Northern Ireland, Scotland and Wales: Lessons for England*, London: The King's Fund

Hardiker, P., Exton, K. and Barker, M. (1991) *Policies and Practices in Preventive Child Care*, Aldershot: Avebury

Harley, B. (2005) *Family Group Conference Pilot Project in the Foyle Health and Social Services Trust: Evaluation Report*, Londonderry: Foyle Health and Social Services Trust

Hassall, I. (1996) 'Origin and development of family group conferences', in Hudson, J., Morris, A., Maxwell, G. and Galaway, B. (eds) (1996) *Family Group Conferences: Perspectives on Policy and Practice*, Annandale: The Federation Press, pp. 17–36

Hayes, D. (2000a) *An Evaluation of the Family Group Conference Pilot Project in the Ulster Community and Hospitals Trust*, Newtownards: Ulster Community and Hospitals Trust

Hayes, D. (2000b) 'The use of family group conferences in child protection work: An exploration of professionals' views', *Child Care in Practice*, Vol. 6, No. 2, pp. 124–46

Hayes, D. and Houston, S. (2007) 'Lifeworld, system and family group conferences: Habermas's contribution to discourse in child protection', *British Journal of Social Work*, Vol. 37, No. 6, pp. 987–1006

Hayes, D. and Spratt, T. (2014) 'Child welfare as child protection then and now: What social workers did and continue to do', *British Journal of Social Work*, Vol. 44, No. 3, pp. 615–35

HM Government (2010) *The Foundation Years: Preventing Poor Children Becoming Poor Adults*, London: Cabinet Office

HM Government (2011a) *Early Intervention: Smart Investment, Massive Savings*, London: Cabinet Office

HM Government (2011b) *Early Intervention: The Next Steps*, London: Cabinet Office

Hills, J., Sefton, T. and Stewart, K. (2009) *Towards a More Equal Society*, Bristol: The Policy Press

Holland, S., Scourfield, J., O'Neill, S. and Pithouse, A. (2005) 'Democratising the family and the state? The case of family group conferences in child welfare', *Journal of Social Policy*, Vol. 34, No. 1, pp. 59–77

Hood, A. and Phillips, D. (2015) *Benefit Spending and Reforms: The Coalition Government's Record*, London: Institute for Fiscal Studies

Hoy, M. (unpublished) 'The participation promise of family group conferencing – theory or practice? A qualitative comparison study of children's participation in family group conferences and child protection case conferences', doctoral thesis, Belfast: Queen's University

HSCB (2011a) *Empowering Families: Regional Guidance on the Provision of Family Group Conferences in Health and Social Care Trusts Children and Young People Services*, Belfast: Health and Social Care Board

HSCB (2011b) *Transforming Your Care: A Review of Health and Social Care in Northern Ireland*, Belfast: Health and Social Care Board

Huntsman, L. (2006) *Family Group Conferencing in a Child Welfare Context: A Literature Review,* Ashfield, NSW: Centre for Parenting and Research, Research, Funding and Business Analysis Division, New South Wales Department of Community Services

The Independent (2012) 'Tragic Tetra Pak heiress, Eva Rausing, found dead after lying undiscovered for two months, died of cocaine abuse court hears' (online). Available from URL: www.independent.co.uk/news/uk/home-news/tragic-tetra-pak-heiress-eva-rausing-found-dead-after-lying-undiscovered-for-two-months-died-of-cocaine-abuse-court-hears-8417197.html (accessed 5 February 2015)

Ipsos Mori (2013) *Evaluation of Flying Start: Impact Study*, London: Ipsos Mori

Johnston, H. (2013) *The Social Dimensions of the Crisis: The Evidence and Its Implications*, Report 134, Dublin: National Economic and Social Council

Jones, O. (2011) *Chavs: The Demonization of the Working Class*, London: Verso

Jones, C. and Novak, T. (1993) *Poverty, Welfare and the Disciplinary State*, London: Routledge

Jordan, B. (2001) 'Tough love: Social work, social exclusion and the third way', *British Journal of Social Work*, Vol. 31, No. 4, pp. 527–46

Jordan, B. (2006) *Social Policy for the Twenty-First Century: Big Issues, New Perspectives*, Cambridge: Polity Press

Karoly, L. M., Kilburn, R. and Cannon, J. (2005) *Early Childhood Interventions: Proven Results, Future Promise*, Santa Monica, CA: RAND

Kennan, D., Fives, A. and Canavan, J. (2012) 'Accessing a hard to reach population: Reflections on research with Young Carers in Ireland', *Child and Family Social Work*, Vol. 17, No. 3, pp. 275–83

Kretzmann, J. and McKnight, J. (1993) *Building Communities from the Inside Out; A Path Towards Finding and Mobilizing a Communities Assets*, Evanston, IL: Institute for Policy Research

Lister, R. (2004) *Poverty*, Cambridge: The Policy Press

Local Government Chronicle (1999) 'Launch of Sure Start: Government puts children and the family first' (online). Available at URL: www.lgcplus.com/launch-of-sure-start-government-puts-children-and-the-family-first-and-chancellors-speech/1414254.article (accessed 19 February 2015)

Local Government Chronicle (2006) 'Surer Start for 800,00 children' (online). Available at URL: www.lgcplus.com/surer-start-for-800000-children/499293.article (accessed 20 February 2015)

Local Government Leadership and Westminster City Council (2010) *Repairing Broken Families and Rescuing Fractured Communities: Lessons from the Frontline*, London: Westminster City Council

Lorenz, W. (2006) *Perspectives on European Social Work – From the Birth of the Nation State to the Impact of Glabalization*, Opladen and Farmington Hills, MI: Verlag Barbara Budrich

Lupton, R., Burchardt, T., Fitzgerald, A., Hills, J., McKnight, A., Obolenskaya, P., Stewart, K., Thomson, S., Tunstall, R. and Vizard, P. (2015) *The Coalition's Social Policy Record: Policy, Spending and Outcomes 2010–2015,*

London and Manchester: The Centre for Analysis of Social Exclusion

Luthar, S. and Zelazo, L. B. (2003) 'Resilience and vulnerability: Adaptation in the context of Childhood adversities', in Luthar, S. (ed.) (2003) *Resilience and Vulnerability*, New York: Cambridge University Place

Malik, S. (2012) 'Adoption process will be made fairer and faster, says Cameron' (online). Available from URL: www.theguardian.com/society/2012/mar/09/adoption-made-fairer-faster-cameron (accessed 5 February 2015)

Marsh, P. and Crow, G. (1998) *Family Group Conferences in Child Welfare*, Oxford: Blackwell

McCardle, L. (2014) 'Council considers closing all children's centres' (online). Available from URL: www.cypnow.co.uk/cyp/news/1143562/council-considers-closing-childrens-centres (accessed 5 February 2015)

McCready, A. and Donnelly, A. (2005) *Family Group Conference Project Homefirst Community Trust: Evaluation Report March 2001 to October 2004*, Ballymena: Homefirst Community Trust

McDermid, S. and Holmes, L. (2013) *The Cost Effectiveness of Action for Children's Intensive Family Support Services: Final Report*, Loughborough: Centre for Child and Family Research, Loughborough University

McGinnity, F., Russell, H., Watson, D., Kingston G. and Kelly E. (2014) *Winners and Losers: The Equality Impact of the Great Recession in Ireland*, Dublin: Economic and Social Research Institute

McKenzie, L. (2015) *Estates, Class and Culture in Austerity Britain*, Bristol: The Policy Press

McMahon, L. and Keenan, P. (2008) *NICCY Rights Review 2008*, Belfast: Northern Ireland Commissioner for Children and Young People

Merkel-Holguin, L., Tinworth, K., Horner, A. and Wilmot, L. (2007) 'Using family group conferences to achieve permanency for youth', *Protecting Children*, Vol. 22, No. 1, pp. 38–49

Merrell, C. and Tymms, P. (2011) 'Changes in children's cognitive development at the start of school in England 2001–2008', *Oxford Review of Education*, Vol. 37, No. 3, pp. 333–45

Ministry of Justice (2010) *Breaking the Cycle: Effective Punishment, Rehabilitation and Sentencing of Offenders*, London: Ministry of Justice

Morgan, R. (2004) *Collaboration not Competition, Agenda*, Cardiff: Institute of Welsh Affairs

Morgan, R., (2006) 'Forward', in Day, G., Dunkerley, D. and Thompson, A. (eds) *Civil Society in Wales: Policy, Politics and People*, Cardiff: University of Wales Press

Morris, K. (2012) 'Troubled families: Vulnerable families' experiences of multiple service use', *Child and Family Social Work*, Vol. 18, No. 2, pp. 198–206

Morris, K. and Connolly, M. (2012) 'Family decision-making in child welfare: Challenges in developing a knowledge base for practice', *Child Abuse Review*, Vol. 21, No. 1, pp. 41–52

Mulgan, G. (2008) *Thinker in Residence Report Innovation in 360°: Promoting Social Innovation in South Australia*, Adelaide: Department of the Premier and Cabinet

Mulhern, G. (1996) 'Network conferencing with young people', in Morris, K.

and Tunnard, J. (eds) (1996) *Family Group Conferencing: Messages from UK Practice and Research*, London: Family Rights Group, pp. 31–8

Munro, E. (2011) *The Munro Review of Child Protection: Final Report, A Child-Centred System*, Vol. 8062, London: The Stationery Office

Murray, C. (1990) *The Emerging British Underclass. Choice in Welfare Series, No. 2*, London: Health and Welfare Unit, Institute of Economic Affairs

NCSR (2009) *Antisocial Behaviour Family Intervention Projects: Monitoring and Evaluation: Research Brief*, London: Department for Children, Schools and Families

NESST (2008) *The Impact of Sure Start Local Programmes on Three Year Olds and Their Families*, London: HMSO

NESST (2010) *The Impact of Sure Start Local Programmes on Three Year Olds and Their Families*, London: HMSO

NESST (2012) *The Impact of Sure Start Programmes on Seven Year Olds and their Families*, London: Department for Education. Available from URL: www.ness.bbk.ac.uk/impact/documents/DFE-RR220.pdf (accessed 5 February 2015)

NHS Institute for Innovation and Improvement (2007) *Improvement Leader's Guides*, Coventry: NHS Institute for Innovation and Improvement

NISRA (2014) *Census 2011: Ireland and Northern Ireland*, Belfast: Northern Ireland Statistics and Research Agency/Central Statistics Office

Nixon, J., Parr, S., Hunter, C. *et al.* (2006) *Anti-Social Behaviour Intensive Family Support Projects: An Evaluation of Six Pioneering Projects*, London: Department for Communities and Local Government

NSPCC (2014) *How Safe Are Our Children?* London, National Society for the Prevention of Cruelty to Children

O'Brien, V. (2000) *An Evaluation of the Family Group Conference Pilot Project in the Eastern Health Board*, Dublin: Eastern Regional Health Authority

Office of the Minister for Children (2007) *The Agenda for Children's Services: A Policy Handbook*, Dublin: Office of the Minister for Children, Department of Health and Children

Penn, H. (2007) 'Childcare market management: How the United Kingdom government has reshaped its role in developing early childhood education and care', *Contemporary Issues in Early Childhood*, Vol. 8, No. 3, pp. 192–207

Penn, H. and Gough, D. (2002) 'The price of a loaf of bread: Some conceptions of family support', *Children and Society*, Vol. 16, pp. 17–32

Pennell, J. and Burford, G. (2000) 'Family group decision making: Protecting children and women', *Child Welfare*, Vol. 79, No. 2, pp. 131–58

Pinkerton, J. and Dolan, P. (2007) 'Family support, social capital, resilience and adolescent coping', *Child and Family Social Work*, Vol. 12, No. 3, pp. 219–28

Pithouse, A. (2007) 'Early intervention in the round: A good idea but …', *British Journal of Social Work*, Vol. 38, No. 8, pp. 1536–52

Pithouse, A. (2011) 'Devolution and change since the Children Act 1989: New directions in Wales', *Journal of Children's Services*, Vol. 6, No. 3, pp. 172–85

Price, V. and Simpson, G. (2007) *Transforming Society? Sociology and Social*

Work, Bristol: The Policy Press

Richards, S. (2011) 'Labour's profligacy is a myth that Miliband must debunk (online). Available from URL: www.independent.co.uk/voices/commentators/steve-richards/steve-richards-labours-profligacy-is-a-myth-that-miliband-must-debunk-2181167.html (accessed 5 February 2015)

Rickford, F. (1991) 'The ties that bind', *Social Work Today* (28 November), p. 20

Robson, K. and Savage, A. (2001) 'Assessing adult attachment: Interview course with Patricia Crittenden', *Child Abuse Review,* Vol. 10, pp. 440–7

Robson, K. and Tooby, A. (2004) 'Play therapy with looked after children: An attachment perspective', *British Journal of Play Therapy,* Vol. 1, No. 1, pp. 16–26

Robson, K. and Wetherell, A. (2011) 'The use of the dynamic maturational model of attachment and adaptation within a systemic setting in CAMHS', *Cumbria Partnership Journal of Research Practice and Learning,* Vol. 1, No. 2, pp. 48–52

Rose, W. (2010) 'The assessment framework', in Horwath, J. (ed.) (2010) *The Child's World,* 2nd edn, London: Jessica Kingsley, pp. 34–55

Ryan, S. (2009) *Commission to Inquire into Child Abuse Report,* Vols I–V, Dublin: Stationery Office

Saleeby, D. (2004) *The Strengths Perspective in Social Work Practice,* New York: Longman

Salford City Council (2015) 'Early intervention and prevention service' (online). Available from URL: www.salford.gov.uk/early-intervention-services.htm (accessed 5 February 2015)

Schrader-McMillan, A., Barnes, J. and Barlow, J. (2011) *Evidence on Effectiveness of Interventions (Home, Early Education, Child Care) in Promoting Social and Emotional Wellbeing of Vulnerable Children Under Five,* Coventry: Warwick Medical School, University of Warwick

Schulman, S., Curtis, C. and Vanstone, C. (2011) 'Family by family: A co-designed & co-produced family support model', in Bretting, K. and Sims, M. (eds) (2011) *Building Integrated Connections for Children, Their Families and Communities,* Newcastle on Tyne: Cambridge Scholars Publishing

Scottish Executive (2001) *For Scotland's Children: Better Integrated Children's Services,* Edinburgh: Scottish Executive

Scottish Executive (2002) *It's Everyone's Job To Make Sure I'm Alright: Report of the Child Protection Audit and Review,* Edinburgh: Scottish Executive

Scottish Executive (2004a) *A Curriculum for Excellence – The Curriculum Review,* Edinburgh: Scottish Executive

Scottish Executive (2004b) *Protecting Children and Young People: The Charter,* Edinburgh: Scottish Executive

Scottish Executive (2005a) *Getting it right for every child: Proposals for Action.* Edinburgh: Scottish Executive

Scottish Executive (2005b) *Health for All Children 4: Guidance on Implementation in Scotland,* Edinburgh: Scottish Executive

Scottish Executive (2006) *Getting It Right For Every Child: Implementation Plan,* Edinburgh: Scottish Executive

Scottish Government (2007) *Better Health, Better Care: Action Plan*, Edinburgh: Scottish Government

Scottish Government (2008) *A Guide to Getting It Right For Every Child*, Edinburgh: Scottish Government

Scottish Government (2010a) *Annual Report of the Chief Medical Officer: Health in Scotland 2009, Time for Change*, Edinburgh: Scottish Government

Scottish Government (2010b) *A Guide to Implementing Getting It Right For Every Child: Messages from Pathfinders and Learning Partners*, Edinburgh: Scottish Government

Scottish Government (2012a) *A Guide to Getting It Right For Every Child*, Edinburgh: Scottish Government

Scottish Government (2012b) *Annual Report of the Chief Medical Officer: Health in Scotland 2011, Transforming Scotland's Health*, Edinburgh: Scottish Government

Scottish Government (2013a) *UNCRC: The Foundation of Getting It Right For Every Child*, Edinburgh: Scottish Government

Scottish Government (2013b) *Well-being*, No. 2 (Autumn) (online). Available at URL: www.gov.scot/Topics/People/Young-People/gettingitright (accessed 19 February 2015)

Scottish Government (2014a) *Proposal for the Development of Guidance to Support the GIRFEC Provisions in the Children and Young People (Scotland) Act 2014*, Edinburgh: Scottish Government

Scottish Government (2014b) *Child Poverty Strategy for Scotland: Our Approach 2014–2017*, Edinburgh: Scottish Government

Scottish Government and COSLA (2008) *The Early Years Framework: A Joint Scottish Government and COSLA Policy Statement*, Edinburgh: Scottish Government

Scottish Government and COSLA (2011) *Early Years Framework: Progress So Far*, Edinburgh: Scottish Government

Seddon, J. (2008) *Systems Thinking in the Public Sector*, Axminster: Triarchy Press

Simpson, G. and Connor, S. (2011) *Social Policy for Welfare Professionals: Tools for Understanding, Analysis and Engagement*, Bristol: The Policy Press

Sinclair, R., Hearn, B. and Pugh, G. (1997) *Preventative Work with Families: The Role of Mainstream Services*, London: National Children's Bureau

Social Exclusion Unit (2004) *Creating Sustainable Communities*, London: Office of the Deputy Prime Minister

SQW (2013) *Flying Start: A Qualitative Research with High Need Families*, London: SQW

Stephens, J., Hayes, D. and Holliday, J. (2002) *Evaluation of Diamond House Family Group Conference and School Group Conference Pilot Scheme*, Cardiff: Barnardos

Stradling, B. and MacNeil, M. (2007) *Developing Integrated Services for Children in Highland: An Overview of Challenges, Developments and Outcomes*, Inverness: The Highland Council, NHS Highland and University of the Highlands & Islands Millennium Institute

Stradling, B., MacNeil, M. and Berry, H. (2009) *Changing Professional Practice and Culture to Get It Right For Every Child: An Evaluation of the Development and Early Implementation Phases of Getting It Right For Every Child in Highland: 2006–2009*, Edinburgh: Scottish Government

TACSI (2013) *Mount Druitt Scoping & Start-up Report*, Emerion, NSW: The Australian Centre for Social Innovation. Available from URL: http://tacsi.org.au/co-design-school/Mount_Druitt_Scoping_Report.pdf (accessed 20 January 2015)

Taylor, C., Rhys, M. and Waldron, S. (2013) 'The best start in life: What do we know about the impact of early interventions on children's life chances?', *Evidence Symposium Briefing Paper*, Cardiff: Cardiff University, The Wales Institute of Social and Economic Research, Data and Methods/Economic and Social Research Council

Teggart, T. and Menary, J. (2005). 'An investigation of the mental health needs of children looked after by Craigavon and Banbridge Health and Social Services Trust', *Childcare in Practice*, Vol. 11, No. 1, pp. 39–49

Thistlethwaite, P. (2011) *Integrating Health and Social Care in Torbay*, London: The King's Fund

Time Banking UK (2011) *People Can*, Stroud: Timebanking UK

Titcomb, A. and LeCroy, C. (2005) 'Outcomes of Arizona's family group decision making programme', *Protecting Children*, Vol. 19, No. 4, pp. 47–53

Toynbee, P. (2015) 'Cameron cuts, and the money is recycled to the rich' (online). Available from URL: www.theguardian.com/commentisfree/2015/jan/27/cameron-tax-cuts-voters-labour-austerity (accessed 5 February 2015)

Tunstill, J. and Allnock, S. (2007) *Understanding the Contribution of Sure Start Local Programmes to the Task of Safeguarding Children's Welfare. Research Report: NESS/2007/FR/026*, London: Birkbeck College, National Evaluation of Sure Start Team

UNOCINI (2008) *Understanding the Needs of Children in Northern Ireland: Guidance and Forms*, Belfast: Department of Health, Social Services and Public Safety. Available from URL: www.dhsspsni.gov.uk/index/ssi/oss-childrens-services.htm (accessed 20 January 2015)

Velen, M. and Devine, L. (2005) 'Use of family group decision making with children in care the longest: It's about time', *Protecting Children*, Vol. 19, No. 4, pp. 25–34

Vincent, S. (2010) *Learning from Child Deaths and Serious Abuse in Scotland*, Edinburgh, Dunedin

Vincent, S. (2012) *Preventing Child Deaths: Learning from Review*, Edinburgh, Dunedin

Vincent, S. (2013) *An Analysis of the Impact of the Support Provided by the Area Family Support Teams in Walsall*, Walsall: Walsall Council

Vincent, S. and Simpson, G. (2013) 'Intake and assessment processes in child welfare and protection systems in the United Kingdom, New Zealand, Canada, the United States, Australia, the Netherlands, Germany and Sweden: A paper to inform the NSW program review of intake and assessment', unpublished paper for NSW government

VOYPIC (2007) *Consultation Response: Care Matters in Northern Ireland – A Bridge to a Better Future,* Belfast: Voice of Young People in Care

Waldfogel, J. and Washbrook, E. (2011) 'Early years policy', *Child Development Research*; doi:10.1155/2011/343016

Walsh, C. (2010) 'Youth justice and neuroscience', *British Journal of Criminology*, Vol. 51, No. 1, pp. 21–39

Wastell, D. and White, S. (2012) 'Blinded by neuroscience: Social policy, the family and the infant brain', *Families, Relationships and Society*, Vol. 1, No. 3, pp. 397–414

Weil, S. (1955) *The Need for Roots*, London: Routledge

Welsh Local Government Association (2013) 'Looked-after children'. Available from URL: www.wlga.gov.uk/publications-and-consultation-responses-ss/all-wales-heads-of-childrens-services-research-on-differences-in-the-looked-after-children-population (accessed 20 January 2015)

Western Health Board (1996) *A Child Is Dead: Report of a Committee of Inquiry into the Death of Kelly Fitzgerald*, Dublin: The Stationery Office

Westhorp, G. (2012) *Family by Family Evaluation Report (2011–12)*, Mt Torrens, SA: Community Matters

WG (2013a) *Building a Brighter Future: Early Years and Childcare Plan*, Cardiff: Welsh Government

WG (2013b) *Adoptions, Outcomes and Placements for Children Looked After, Wales 2012–2013*, Cardiff: National Statistics, Welsh Government

WG (2013c) *Referrals, Assessment and Social Services for Children, Wales 2012–2013*, Cardiff: National Statistics, Welsh Government

WG (2013d) *Welsh Government Response to the Children's Commissioner's Annual Report 2012/2013*, Cardiff: Welsh Government

WG (2013e) *Flying Start Qualitative Research with High Needs Families*, Social Research 64/2013, Cardiff: Welsh Government

WG (2013f) 'Families first' (online). Available from URL: http://wales.gov.uk/topics/people-and-communities/people/children-and-young-people/parenting-support-guidance/help/familiesfirst/?lang=en (accessed 19 February 2015)

WG (2013g) 'Welsh government determined to help most vulnerable families' (online). Available from URL: http://wales.gov.uk/newsroom/firstminister/2013/130130ff/?lang=en (accessed 19 February 2015)

WG (2013h) *Evaluation of Families First: Year One Report*, Social Research 80/2013, Cardiff: Welsh Government

WG (2014a) *Social Services Statistics Wales 2012–13*, Cardiff, Statistics for Wales, Welsh Government

WG (2014b) *Data Linking Demonstration Project – Flying Start*, Cardiff: Social Research, Welsh Government

Wheeler, B. (2013) 'Louise Casey: Social workers "collude" with problem families' (online). Available from URL: www.bbc.co.uk/news/uk-politics-23158680 (accessed 5 February 2015)

WHO (1997) *Life Skills Education for Children and Adolescents in Schools: Introduction and Guidelines to Facilitate the Development and*

Implementation of Life Skills Programmes, Geneva: World Health Organization Programme on Mental Health

Wilmot, L. (2000) 'It's not too late: The use of family group decision making processes to achieve family reunification', *Protecting Children,* Vol. 16, No. 3, pp. 34–8

Wintour, P. (2013) 'Eric Pickles hails progress in tackling "troubled families" (online). Available from URL: www.theguardian.com/society/2013/nov/25/problem-families-department-for-communities (accessed 20 January 2015)

INDEX